MAN

CW00548500

A SHORT (_ _ . _ . . . _
DIGITAL AGE

Recruiting, selecting, retaining and developing great people are essential for any successful business. And the combination of digital transformation and post-pandemic work realities presents major challenges for all organisations. This book provides best practice talent management guidance for businesses undertaking digital transformation or facing digital disruption.

Taking the reader through the stages of talent acquisition, selection, retention and development, this practical and concise book:

- sets out, assesses and predicts how the digital revolution impacts talent management practices, and helps the reader navigate the journey from an analogue to a digital organisation;
- updates talent management concepts and illustrates these with examples and cases of best practice across the business world; and
- enables senior leaders, talent management professionals and managers to quickly access and implement key learnings through the use of practitioner point summaries and a set of Ten Top Tips in each relevant chapter.

The book provides practical insights, grounded in research, into how to manage talent in a fluid and dynamic world of digital change and is aimed at senior leaders and managers, and the HR community. It clearly shows how organisations undertaking a digital journey need to flex and adapt their talent management processes.

Mike Rugg-Gunn is a chartered occupational psychologist and an associate fellow of the British Psychological Society. Mike is married with two adult children and lives in Suffolk, UK.

MANAGING TALENT

A SHORT GUIDE FOR
THE DIGITAL AGE

Mike Rugg-Gunn

Routledge
Taylor & Francis Group

LONDON AND NEW YORK

Designed cover image: Getty Images / DKosig

First published 2024
by Routledge
4 Park Square, Milton Park, Abingdon, Oxon OX14 4RN

and by Routledge
605 Third Avenue, New York, NY 10158

Routledge is an imprint of the Taylor & Francis Group, an informa business

British Library Cataloguing-in-Publication Data
A catalogue record for this book is available from the British Library

Library of Congress Cataloging-in-Publication Data
Names: Rugg-Gunn, Mike, author.
Title: Managing talent : a short guide for the digital age / Mike Rugg-Gunn.
Description: Abingdon, Oxon ; New York, NY : Routledge, 2023. | Includes bibliographical references and index. |
Identifiers: LCCN 2022060532 (print) | LCCN 2022060533 (ebook) | ISBN 9781032389974 (hardback) | ISBN 9781032394114 (paperback) | ISBN 9781003349587 (ebook)
Subjects: LCSH: Personnel management. | Digital media. | Ability.
Classification: LCC HF5549.A3 R84 2023 (print) | LCC HF5549.A3 (ebook) | DDC 658.300285--dc23/eng/20230421
LC record available at https://lccn.loc.gov/2022060532
LC ebook record available at https://lccn.loc.gov/2022060533

ISBN: 978-1-032-38997-4 (hbk)
ISBN: 978-1-032-39411-4 (pbk)
ISBN: 978-1-003-34958-7 (ebk)

DOI: 10.4324/9781003349587

Typeset in Bembo
by Taylor & Francis Books

This book is dedicated to our granddaughter, Scarlett.
May she live, work and thrive in this brave new world.

CONTENTS

ILLUSTRATIONS

BOXES

ACKNOWLEDGEMENTS

Although this book is a short guide, it would have been impossible without the help of many friends, colleagues and professional associates who have offered much helpful feedback and support across all stages of the production.

My special thanks to Adam Gordon, Amanda Smithson, Carole Miles, Danni Clements, Fons Trompenaars, Frank Akoto, Hannah Carroll, Jody Ford, Louise Smith, Marc Effron, Michael Motley, Peter Plumb, Simon Davidson, Sophie Martin and Val Srivanas for all their assistance. To Lauren Whelan, Nicole Wiles and Rebecca Marsh from Routledge for their guidance, support, positivity and optimism. And to my wife, Sue, who has encouraged me to write this book for a number of years; my daughter, Fiona, and daughter-in-law, Gem, for their supportive feedback on early scripts.

Any omissions, errors or inconsistencies are irrevocably mine, all mine and mine alone.

INTRODUCTION

'People are our greatest asset' is a hackneyed phrase repeated across many annual reports and is intended to stress that people play a key role in executing the business strategy. That much is true, but it masks the fact that it is less about people per se and much more about how they are recruited, selected, developed and retained across the business. In short, it is about the science of talent management.

The notion of talent management has been around for thousands of years, as humans have sought to work collaboratively to both survive and thrive in their communities through allocating important tasks according to specific skill sets. In 207 BC, in ancient China, the civil service was formed by Emperor Gaozu, who recognised that he needed well-educated ministers to run the empire for him. Selection for these prestigious roles was through complex examination. Fast forward to 2001, and the publication of *The War for Talent* book,[1] articulated in its title a phrase that many employers recognised, grappling as they were with issues of recruitment and retention in the face of intense competition for the best and brightest against the backdrop of a declining demographic population. Although, this book became an international bestseller, there were several criticisms.[2] Predominant among these was the explicit link between five imperatives of managing talent and superior corporate performance, with several commentators casting doubt on the medium-to-long-term performance of the exemplar companies, of which Enron was one.

Since then, there has been a burgeoning number of print and online publications in talent management, to the extent that it

DOI: 10.4324/9781003349587-1

has become a profession in its own right, sometimes working as part of an expanded human resource (HR) function and sometimes in place of it. Whatever the nature of the change, all senior leaders, HR and talent management professionals need to be acutely aware that the digital revolution will swamp them like a tsunami unless they are fully prepared, ready and excited to meet the challenges to their business that this transformation will yield.

The fourth industrial revolution is upon us and will result in profound changes in the world of work across the globe. Digitisation is breaking down barriers across businesses, rewriting long-held management theories about competition, strategy, creativity, data analytics and business model innovation, to name just a few. Such change, however, is rendered worthless without talented people to deliver it. This book explores how organisations can adapt their talent management strategies and practices to address the new realities of the digital revolution.

If the situation was not complex enough for business leaders, then this was further compounded by COVID-19. The pandemic that started in 2020 had a catalytic effect on digital transformation across the globe. One area where this is most obvious is that of remote working, with many millions of people working from home, using video conferencing facilities to conduct their work. An original assumption was that this was a temporary measure until 'normality' returned, but the die is cast: there will be no return to pre-pandemic ways of working. In a more holistic sense, the pandemic has developed the relationship between humans and technology and enabled recruitment to cross boundaries. Talented people now have a choice not just about what they do and where they work, but about how they work and where they live to do it.

The business context is changing, and Chapter One explores this in detail – in particular, the rise of artificial intelligence; the nature of digital disruption and transformation; the impact of the pandemic, the changing nature of work and the implications of these factors for a company's strategy, culture and business model; and how these influence talent management strategies.

Post-pandemic talent shortages across the globe dictate that businesses need to be very aware of how they market their attractiveness to talented people, and this is explored further in Recruitment (Chapter Two). New technologies impact Selection (Chapter Three), with numerous online assessment products now available on the market. Leaders are encouraged to remain dispassionate with those suppliers who flaunt their technological prowess but whose tools lack evidence of reliability, validity and fairness. Post-pandemic, many businesses, across the globe, have struggled to retain talented employees. Retention (Chapter Four) explores how motivation, goal setting, feedback and performance management impact retention. Development (Chapter Five) considers psychological theories of applied human learning and their relevance to the acquisition and dissemination of digital skills and knowledge across the business. Finally, there are profound implications for members of the HR profession for how they structure and organise themselves to address this fast-changing landscape and stay ahead of the business growth curve with talent strategies to match. Chapter Six explores these issues in depth and looks into the future for talent management.

The growing gap between science and practice is a cause for concern. For example, research in such topics as online selection tools now lags commercial implementation by several years. Some commentators suggest that we know all we need to know about talent management, and the challenge is to apply the principles effectively. This viewpoint is rejected. The onrush of digital transformation and the COVID-19 pandemic have combined to change industry dynamics and impact corporate strategies for ever. By implication, talent management theories must adapt and change to respond appropriately. Within this context, this book has four primary objectives:

Objective 1 is to set out, understand, assess and predict how the digital revolution impacts talent management practices.

Part of this objective is to provide an update on the science that does exist and is of direct relevance to talent management. A seminal article[3] by both practitioners and academics on this subject highlights the need to maintain a watching brief on new developments and to look across disciplines (especially technology) to help gain a broader perspective and ensure a greater relevance to practitioners. This is not as easy as it may sound, as there is much 'science' out there that is not science at all, and this cues us to the next objective.

Objective 2 is to update talent management theories that are rooted in bona fide research and to illustrate these with practical examples of best practice across the business world. In this way, the book sets out to bridge some of the academic–practitioner divide.

Objective 3 is to ensure that senior leaders, talent management professionals and others can quickly access and implement key learnings. The end of each chapter will contain a summary of practitioner points and Ten Top Tips in the form of a checklist.

During 2020, there has been a renewed awakening around issues of diversity and inclusion (D&I). The book does not contain a specific chapter on this, but it will note the (mostly positive) impact that modern technologies have on equality issues in talent management, and this will be a recurring theme throughout the book.

Objective 4 is to inform how talent management practices ensure that all people from diverse backgrounds feel valued in their workplace and work in an inclusive culture that enables them to give of their best and achieve their career goals.

REFERENCES

1 : Michaels, E., Handfield-Jones, H. & Axelrod, B., 2001. *The war for talent.* Harvard Business Press.

2: Munro, A., 2013. What happened to the war for talent exemplars? Available at www.slideshare.net/AndrewMunro/what-happenedtothewarforta lentexemplars. Accessed 14 January 2021.

3: Rotolo, C. T., Church, A.H., Adler, S., Smither, J.W., Colquitt, A.L., Shull, A.C., Paul, K. B. & Foster, G., 2018. Putting an end to bad talent management: a call to action for the field of industrial and organizational psychology. *Industrial and Organizational Psychology*, 11(2), 176–219.

THE BUSINESS CONTEXT

INTRODUCTION

Talent management, like any other human resource initiative, does not sit in isolation from the rest of the organisation. It is impacted by the prevailing business context. This is fundamental when defining both the talent management strategy and the operational activities that will deliver it. As such, this chapter will:

- examine the relationship between talent management and financial performance
- explore the technological and socio-cultural factors that impact talent management
- discuss the digital revolution and the changing nature of business strategy for digital enterprises
- recognise the importance of culture as an enabler of the strategy
- understand the shifting nature of business model innovations and their relevance to businesses undergoing digital transformation

TALENT MANAGEMENT: WHY BOTHER?

Although there is much evidence linking talent management practices to several positive outcomes (e.g., employee satisfaction and motivation), one criticism of talent management is that it has been slow to show a clear relationship between superior talent management and financial performance. *The War for*

DOI: 10.4324/9781003349587-2

Talent book[1] suggested that employing the best talent, paying them more, differentiating them and developing them would lead to improved business results. The difficulty here is that the relationship between effective talent management practices and superior company performance is more complex, as there are any other number of variables that also contribute to effective corporate performance. It would require equally complex statistical processes to isolate these.

Some research[2] had sought to understand how the strategic capabilities of firms align with the talent of senior leaders to impact financial performance, expressed in terms of total returns to shareholders (TRS). In extensive research in 200 companies, the researchers divided firms into winners, losers, climbers and tumblers, based on their TRS over a ten-year time frame. Their analyses suggested four foundation clusters comprising, strategy, structure, culture and execution. Simply possessing these four clusters was not enough to attain winner status, but, when these were combined with any two from four additional capabilities (leadership, innovation, growth and talent), then winner status was secured.

The key learning from this research is that talent on its own cannot deliver financial performance. It is how talent builds and sustains the four foundation clusters that leads to superior performance. In this sense, talent is a mediating, but nonetheless important, variable in delivering this. This research also supports the growth of data analytics to inform talent management strategies. This is a fast-emerging science, as senior leaders seek to drive their decisions using scientific data and processes, that forms part of a broader-based approach towards evidence-based management.

EXTERNAL AND INTERNAL FACTORS IMPACTING TALENT MANAGEMENT

Talent management is impacted by external factors such as technological and socio-cultural issues and internally by the firm's strategy, culture and prevailing business model. These critical factors are now considered in turn.

TECHNOLOGICAL

THE RISE AND RISE OF ARTIFICIAL INTELLIGENCE (AI)

AI is the science and engineering of making intelligent machines. There are several articles[3] and bodies of research that describe human-level AI in greater detail. To paraphrase these, AI is impacting lives in many ways, and there is no part of talent management in which it does not have a major influence. For example, in recruitment (Chapter Two), AI and other machine learning technologies are working swiftly to reduce hiring costs through automating tasks, thus freeing up recruiters to perform other functions that only a human can do. Similarly, in selection, (Chapter Three), it is used to automate any number of high-volume assessment processes to drive down costs. In retention (Chapter Four), it is used to measure employee activity and performance and produce data to predict voluntary exits. Finally, AI is also making a fundamental difference to learning and development options (Chapter Five) through personalising learning pathways based on machine learning that analyses the impact of different learning content.

AI is not without its critics. Chief among these are concerned with its ethical use so that it creates useful rather than harmful outcomes for both individuals and organisations. In short, companies need to adopt a responsible approach to using this technology. International bodies such as the European Union (EU) recognise this – hence the creation of the General Data Protection Regulation (2018) to protect the privacy of its citizens. This requires at the very least a board-level understanding of compliance best practices.[4] This concept of the ethical use of AI will be developed further across the respective chapters.

Furthermore, there are challenges to the concepts of diversity and inclusion represented in AI. For example, some facial recognition operations have different outcomes across ethnic groups, and some word embedding mechanisms (used in many natural language processing tools) display bias against intersectional groups. Research[5] proposes a four-point plan as a solution to counter bias in AI applications. These include being intentional about looking at the ways that diversity variables (e.g., age, ethnicity, race and gender identity) may be disadvantaged by the application of current AI tools; next, using bona fide statistical techniques to evaluate performance across these differing groups; then, using these data to highlight how improvements can be made to AI to minimise bias; and, finally, designing a statistical model that fixes the problems.

BIG DATA AS A STRATEGIC ASSET

Bigger volumes of data now traverse the internet every second than were stored across the whole internet 20 years ago. These allow leaders to make quicker and smarter decisions, and the ability to harness and manipulate data to reveal patterns and trends can deliver significant competitive advantage. The digital revolution has focused attention on how such data are collected, harnessed, stored and analysed. Table 1.1[6] sets out changes in assumptions about data as businesses move into the digital age.

Table 1.1 Data changes in strategic assumptions from the analogue to the digital age

Old	New
It is expensive for a business to generate data	Data are continuously generated everywhere
Challenges of data concern storage and management	Challenge of data is converting them into valid and reliable information
Businesses use only structured data	Unstructured data are increasingly usable and generate value
Data are managed in operational silos	Value of data lies in connection across silos
Data are a tool for optimising processes	Data are a key intangible asset for value creation

Source: Rogers, D., 2016. *The Digital Transformation Playbook* (Chapter 4, p. 91). Columbia University Press.

All this requires treating data as a strategic asset and thus setting out a strategy for how to gather the right data and then deploy them to generate long-term business value. A data strategy is thus a long-term guiding plan that identifies and harnesses people, processes and technologies that need to be in place to resolve the business's data problems. In short, the creation of a data strategy enables big data to be identified, collected, collated, warehoused and democratised so that all who need them have clear access as and when they need them.

Big data are unstructured data (i.e., they are recorded but unformed). The growth of social media is a prime example of this. This diversification of data sources should be welcomed by boards, but they need help to synthesise these new data assets into digestible chunks, such as dashboards or score cards, which can aid decision making. These sorts of tools should enable leadership teams to progress their analyses from hindsight (using descriptive analytics), through insight (using diagnostic analytics), towards foresight (using predictive and prescriptive analytics). In short, leadership teams and boards should spend less time talking about the past and more time debating the future as big data and advanced analytical techniques become more robust. This is shown graphically in Figure 1.1.[7]

Types of Data Analytics

Figure 1.1 Gartner® analytic ascendancy model
GARTNER is a registered trademark and service mark of Gartner, Inc. and/or its affiliates in the USA and internationally and is used herein with permission. All rights reserved.
Source: Gartner, *Hiring Trends for Predictive Analytics Competencies in Quality*, Quality Research Team, 16 June 2022.

PEOPLE ANALYTICS

Talent management is not immune to the onslaught of big data. This has led to a burgeoning increase in the study of people analytics. This is a data-driven approach to managing people at work. Compared with data generated by other functions, such as marketing and production, the use of people analytics is a new science. It has not enjoyed a speedy uptake among HR teams, with some feeling that it leads businesses to view people as numbers rather than fellow human beings. The predictive nature of people analytic data is explored further in Chapter Four. There can be little doubt that the deployment of robust people analytic data can only enhance the reputation of an HR team as a strategic business partner.

THE DIGITAL REVOLUTION

An analysis of FTSE 100 firms from the start of 2010 to the end of 2019[8] found that, by sector, technology firms led the way, with an average annual growth rate of 18.1% – some way ahead of other sectors such as telecoms (5.4%), financials (5.2%) and oil and gas (5.1%). More globally, in 2021, Tesla achieved a market capitalisation of more than $1tn, while Apple more than doubled that with a $2.5tn market capitalisation. Across the globe, companies who were traditional bastions of their market sector were finding these positions severely threated by nimbler, leaner digital businesses. For example, Intercontinental Hotel Group is a long-standing, leading hotel company operating 6000 hotels worldwide and with an army of support staff to maintain brand standards. Yet it has a market capitalisation barely 13% of Airbnb's, founded in 2008, which owns no hotels and thus employs no such support staff. These data reflect the rate and pace of technological change. As such, tenure of firms in the UK FTSE 100 is now much shorter than ever before.

DIGITAL DISRUPTION AND DIGITAL TRANSFORMATION: WHAT IS THE DIFFERENCE?

The notion of disruption is not new. Clayton Christensen, writing in 1997,[9] noted that transformation has two opposites –

disruptive technologies and sustaining technologies. Firms using disruption technologies enter the market in the cheaper sectors that have often been abandoned by larger firms that have lost sight of the customer through overly focusing on the competition. The new entrants produce goods that are cheaper and easier to use and, over time, move up through the market segments to chomp away at the existing business's customer base. The example of Blockbuster and Netflix shows how Netflix disrupted Blockbuster's video rental market through the new concept of video streaming. Netflix entered at the bottom of the market to rise quickly, driving Blockbuster into bankruptcy in 2010 when, just two years earlier, its CEO had famously asserted that Netflix is not 'even on the radar screen in terms of competition.'

Sustaining technologies, on the other hand, are focused on improving the performance of the established product range across those areas of performance that customers have traditionally valued. As such, they make incremental improvements to, rather than dramatic shifts in, company performance. This is not to damn them with faint praise, as the data are clear that even the most radical of sustaining technologies rarely lead to failure of leading firms. Some change, it seems, is better than no change at all.

Definitions of digital disruption and transformation follow similar lines. Sometimes, these terms have been used interchangeably. There is, however, a clear difference between the two. One definition of disruption is as follows: 'disruption happens when an existing industry faces a challenger that offers greater value to the customer in a way that existing firms cannot compete with directly.'[6] And digital transformation is 'the evolving pursuit of innovative and agile business and operational models − fuelled by evolving technologies, processes, analytics, and talent − to create new value and experiences for customers, employees, and stakeholders.'[10] Examples of genuine disruption include Airbnb, Uber and ASOS. These businesses adopted emerging digital technologies and business models that disrupted the current market. Thus, although digital transformation is increasingly commonplace, genuine digital disruption is comparatively rare. This is because the intellectual horsepower to envision turning products into platforms and developing ecosystems and new delivery channels involves much complexity. Kodak invented the digital camera but never progressed the innovation, fearing that it might cannibalise their existing products and markets. It filed for Chapter 11 bankruptcy 30 years later. One reason for this collapse was that senior leaders were rooted in the comfort zone of a prevailing mindset and were unable, or unwilling, to embrace the complexities of an alternative business paradigm. In this instance, their inability to accept this new market reality was first and foremost an intellectual issue before it ever became a technological one.[11]

SOCIO-CULTURAL

COVID-19 AND THE CHANGING NATURE OF WORK

The pandemic that began in 2020 has had a catalytic effect on digital transformation across the globe. This has resulted in a paradigm shift in human behaviour, for both consumers and employees.[12] For example, consumer behaviour that was predicted to change over years happened in a matter of months. And there is no going back. How consumers get information and where, what and how they purchase goods and services have changed forever. The world of work has changed forever too. Many companies are now redesigning roles to accommodate the advantages of automated work practices.

As such, work designed to deliver in steady-state environments is being displaced by new environments that are much more flexible, responsive and adaptable. This is clearly visible in two areas. First, in business model innovation, which is discussed later in this chapter, but also in the Agile work paradigm, which is discussed in further detail in Chapter Four. All this has clear implications for organisational design, with some commentators[13] promoting different models to address post-pandemic realities.

For employees, the most obvious implication is the transition to remote working, with millions of people using video conferencing facilities to collaborate and orchestrate work from home that was previously executed in an office. This move has had knock-on effects on other aspects of employee motivation, with workers enjoying the extra time that not commuting has given back to them and seeking roles that are closer to home. This brings into sharp focus how organisations blend the best aspects of co-located and remote working. Thus, the 'new normal' now requires a rethink of both the workforce and its workplace, with the twin aims of increasing interpersonal connection (which, as humans, we both need and value) and enhancing productivity (to ensure the continued survival of the business). This has some positive implications for how talent is managed. For example, where employment is not restricted to a particular location, this increases the opportunities for those more geographically dispersed to gain meaningful employment. This, in turn, must have a positive effect on diversity and inclusion strategies as a wider range of diverse talents become available to hire.

Finally, the pandemic has delivered an enhanced awareness of mental health issues. Government actions such as social distancing and business requirements for remote working can lead to increased feelings of isolation, loneliness and helplessness that in turn lead to stress and anxiety. This is further compounded for working parents who have had to balance their work responsibilities with parental duties (especially during term-time school closures). This has substantial implications for both men and women, but especially the latter as they are often expected to do the domestic chores even if they are paid similarly to their male counterparts.[14] Where once employees might have been reluctant to share mental health worries with their employers, the climate has now changed, with many organisations putting in place well-being initiatives such as employee assistance programmes to support employees in times of difficulty. This, in turn, generates a much sharper focus on leaders' duty of care to ensure the psychological safety of those who work for them.

THE RISE OF THE 'GIG' ECONOMY

There have now been significant changes in how talent is defined. Gone are the days when it was just about those on the company payroll. The gig economy is founded on flexible, freelance or temporary roles, frequently involving connection with customers through an online platform. The trend is thus to view the talent pool in a much wider context, to include, for example, gig economy workers, IT developers and crowd-sourced contributors. This is because the move to platforms over products is developed by specialist knowledge workers who deliver a project over a specific period for an agreed rate. Thus, for the HR professional, workforce planning has become more complex.

This poses several challenges for HR teams. These range from compliance issues such as tax legislation and employment status to the operational imperatives of deciding on the optimal mix of permanent and temporary workers. And who owns this agenda? Is it the functional teams who employ freelance workers or the HR team? If the former, how is HR expected to manage talent in a holistic and integrated fashion? One solution to these conundrums can be found in the creation of workforce eco systems.[15] Rather than ask 'how can our workforce deliver the strategy?' the question is reversed to now ask 'what should be our strategy given the quality, availability, and cost of our current talent pool?' This talent pool is now defined as a cohort of independent operators working both internally and externally to the organisation and delivering on both individual and collective goals. As such, they need to be culturalised, trained and developed with the same level of rigour as would apply to the fully employed workforce. This broadening of the talent definition has profound implications for all aspects of talent management and is a recurring theme across this book.

These fundamental shifts in how to execute work suggest equally fundamental shifts in how leaders need to manage those who work for them. Leaders must adopt differing skills to lead teams remotely and forge trust and a positive group dynamic across teams who rarely meet. They will need to work harder to foster a feeling of inclusion. This is because much of work is now dispersed across different locations, geographies and time zones and is frequently conducted in teams, making it tough for leaders to assess team members' individual contributions and make wider assessments of competence and confidence. Chapter Three discusses how leadership behaviours need to change to address the new realities of leading teams in the digital age.

Chapter Four discusses how new performance management systems and processes complement these behaviours and offer leaders and team members continuous feedback on performance in real time.

BUSINESS STRATEGY FOR DIGITAL BUSINESSES

These technological and socio-cultural factors matter because they fundamentally impact the business strategy. Since the 1980s, Michael Porter's theories have been the prevailing paradigm in business strategy. More especially, his five forces model [16] has been a widely used tool for analysing a firm's competitive advantage. The arrival of the digital era has broken down barriers between industries, and thus the notion of competition is much more complex. Many of the same principles of competitive forces still apply, but they work differently for platforms than for products. The forces exerted by network effects, the creation of ecosystems and rules of access and engagement have radically altered the concept of business strategy. In pipeline businesses, the five forces are clearly defined and stable. In platform businesses, however, things are much less explicit, and competitive threats may emerge from several sources.

All this represents a watershed in thinking about how strategy is conceptualised and is summarised well in a seminal article by van Alstyne et al.[17] Platform businesses that bring together producers and consumers are transforming the rules of competition, leaving those businesses that struggle to create platforms trailing in their wake. In this sense, the central focus of business strategy morphs from controlling and organising internal resources towards creating and sparking external interactions – for example, creating a two-way customer conversation that leverages customers as a resource to generate valuable user content and provide a consistent stream of product development ideas. That, in turn, deploys marketing to inspire purchase through platforms that deliver tailored promotions that personalise the relationship and inspire loyalty and advocacy. These fundamental shifts have clear and obvious implications for the behaviours that senior leaders now need to show in the digital domain.

DIGITAL STRATEGIES

The rules of business strategy are changing, and the implications for talent management are considerable, not least the need to adopt new leadership styles as they start the conversion process from pipelines to platforms. The notion that the talent management strategy should be aligned with the overarching corporate strategy is a logical one, but this is not always easily attained. This is because, as noted above, any talent strategy is only ever going to be a good as the quality and quantity of talent available. The more complex the business and the more it relies on superior knowledge or cognitive skills, then the harder it becomes to attract and retain the required level of talent. As such, there is a trade-off between the aspirations of the business strategy and the probability of attracting the required talent to execute it. The emphasis now moves on to companies thinking carefully about the strategies available to them.[18] Senior leaders need to reconcile heady ambitions with practical realities; those companies that can function and operate as global pure-play disruptors (such as Netflix) are few. Thus, most business should select different strategic paths.

Researchers[19] who were intrigued by the differing speeds at which organisations were adopting digital technologies conducted research to understand better how organisations were deploying digital technologies within their businesses. Their conclusions suggested that it was not just what they invested in, but also how they led the change that enabled these companies to achieve the optimal status of 'digital masters.' Figure 1.2 shows how those companies that excel deliver in two key areas: the 'what' of technology (digital capabilities) and the 'how' of leading change (leadership capabilities). In the former, leaders use technology to change the way that business is conducted through embracing new tools such as social media and data analytics. In the latter, leadership is the 'lever that turns technology into transformation.' Interestingly, the leaders of digital masters were not working to a consensus; they were steering the business with clear direction and maintaining momentum through robust execution.

	FASHIONISTAS	DIGITAL MASTERS
DIGITAL CAPABILITY	**FASHIONISTAS** • Many advanced digital features (e.g., social, mobile) in silos • No overarching vision • Underdeveloped coordination • Digital culture may exist in silos	**DIGITAL MASTERS** • Strong overarching digital vision • Excellent governance across silos • Many digital initiatives generating business value in measurable ways • Strong digital culture
	BEGINNERS • Management sceptical of the business value of advanced digital technologies • May be carrying out some experiments • Immature digital culture	**CONSERVATIVES** • Overarching digital vision, but may be underdeveloped • Few advanced digital features, though traditional digital capabilities may be mature • Strong digital governance across silos • Active steps to build skills and culture
	LEADERSHIP CAPABILITY	

Figure 1.2 What is your level of digital mastery?
Source: *George Westerman, Claire Calmejane, Didier Bonnet, Patrick Ferraris, and Andrew McAfee. 'Digital Transformation: A Roadmap for Billion-Dollar Organisations.'* Cap Gemini Consulting and MIT Centre for Digital Businesses. November 2011.

The model in Figure 1.2 is helpful because it allows businesses to understand where they are on their digital journey. To expand it further:

• beginners believe that they should be doing something but want to see what others are doing before they act; their competitors are silently and stealthily overtaking them
• fashionistas are much more dynamic; they enjoy the bells and whistles of modern technology but have no overarching vision to ensure these are deployed effectively
• conservatives put a toe in the water but are reticent to invest either financially or emotionally in the commitment to new digital technologies; they enjoy useful leadership capability, but their caution will erode stakeholder confidence – talented people will leave

- digital masters: these companies and their leadership teams have achieved market-leading status through fusing investment in digital capability with the mechanics of leading change to deliver significant competitive advantage for the short to medium term, at least until competitors awaken

This model begs the question, 'how do organisations manage their talent on their journey towards digital mastery?' In short, what is the process of workforce planning? For Netflix,[20] the focus was on hiring the team that it wished to have for the future rather than hiring for now. Netflix was sceptical about the potential of existing employees to address the demands of tomorrow rather than doing the same job that they were currently doing. It asked the question, 'do we have enough capacity builders (those who know how to build an effective team) starting with a sharp vision for the future?' And it then identified the knowledge, skills and abilities needed to execute that. It used a sporting analogy where leaders were continually scouting for new talent. If, having assessed internal talent, they concluded that the role required external talent to deliver it optimally, then they had no hesitation in doing this. Key to this is the Netflix employee contract, which made it clear that it was not a career management company. Careers were to be self-managed. Employees, both current and prospective, would have been expected to have understood this culture at the outset and thus were attuned to the probability of external appointments.

DEVELOPING A TALENT MANAGEMENT STRATEGY

In a much broader sense, this calls for a talent management strategy to be future focused, aspirational (in terms of both performance and behaviours) and aligned with both the strategy and culture of the business. Any talent management strategy needs to address several differing perspectives to ensure that talent initiatives are targeted correctly.[21]

INCLUSIVE OR EXCLUSIVE?

First of these is to decide if the organisation should adopt an inclusive (everyone in the organisation is considered as 'talent') or exclusive (a specific focus on 'highflyers') policy? *The War for Talent* was specific in advocating a differentiated and thus exclusive approach to talent. The eventual choice will be culturally formative and thus should not be made lightly. One of the factors leaning towards an exclusive approach is a focus on pivotal positions in the business. These roles are frequently at the intersection of the customer and technology and are critical for business success; it must make sense to prioritise investment in these roles. This is because developmental investment is a scarce resource and should be invested in those people or roles that will deliver the best return.

INNATE OR ACQUIRED?

This has significant implications for talent management practices. Put simply, where is the inflection point between developmental investment and importing the skills required? As noted in the example of Netflix above, the business context and prevailing culture will determine most of the answer to this question. There may be some clearly defined skill shortages where the need to acquire externally becomes paramount. However, learning and development have a clear role to play in enabling people to become more effective in their work, and this is discussed in much further detail in Chapter Five.

INPUT OR OUTPUT PERSPECTIVES?

Finally, the input/output perspective assesses whether talent is dependent on motivation or ability. Input focuses mostly on the former and describes emotional facets such as discretionary effort, motivation and career ambition. The output perspective focuses on external performance measures such as achievements and results. This should not be an either/or dilemma. Both input and output factors contribute equally to the pithy equation that talent = competence × commitment × contribution.[22]

MOVING FROM STRATEGY TO TACTICS AND THE ROLE OF A TALENT MANAGEMENT PHILOSOPHY

Every strategy is defined by its implementation. Indeed, there is a notion among the talent management community that too much attention is accorded to the concept of strategy and not enough to its practical implementation. The idea of a talent philosophy[23] has emerged that seeks to bridge the gap between the talent management strategy and its execution by facilitating senior leadership teams to come together to discuss and agree 'the rules of the road,' or core principles and behaviours for strategy implementation. A talent philosophy suggests that a company's approach to managing talent is defined by five core principles. Table 1.2 outlines these principles and provides a recommended question to debate among the team. Sample responses are shown in the right-hand column.

Table 1.2 Principles for creating a talent philosophy and a sample response

Principle	Sample response
Performance: how long is it okay to be an average 50th-percentile performer in your organisation today? How long should it be in the future?	We believe in strong, sustained performance from all employees; we hold those in critical roles to a higher performance standard
Behaviours: to what extent do a manager's behaviours influence their career progress and compensation today? How much should they in the future?	An individual's behaviours meaningfully influence how they are compensated and their ability to move forward in our company
Differentiation: how much more do we invest in a high-potential leader compared with an average-potential leader? What should this difference be in the future?	Those at the highest level of performance will receive significantly higher rewards than those with average performance

Principle	Sample response
Transparency: how transparent are we today with employees about their career potential within our organisation? How transparent should we be?	We share information with employees about how far and how fast they can advance in our company
Accountability: how accountable are managers for building the quality and depth of their teams? How accountable should they be in the future?	Managers are accountable for building the quality and depth of their team, improving the company's capacity to win

Source: Effron, M., 2020. What's Your Talent Philosophy? The Talent Strategy Group. Available at https://talentstrategygroup.com/whats-your-talent-philosophy-the-original-article-observations-after-five-years/. Accessed 4 July 2022.

This is a useful tool to focus senior leaders' attention on the talent agenda and on using a workshop format collectively to deliver meaningful outputs. There are some key points to note. Just how aligned is the proposed talent philosophy with the prevailing culture? Next, are these just glib responses, or will they really 'live' in the business? One answer to the latter point is to convert these into clearly observable behaviours that now become the language of effective performance across the business. This will also provide a useful behavioural framework for performance management. Aspiring leaders now have a benchmark against which to assess their own behaviours and self-determine those that they need to shed, acquire or retain to be both effective in role and achieve their career aims.

CULTURE MATTERS

'Culture eats strategy for breakfast' is an aphorism attributed to Peter Drucker. It reiterates the view that, while an organisation might have developed the most compelling strategy, it is worthless without the culture that enables it. This stresses the importance of people to the business. If their hearts and minds, motivations and desires are not fully engaged, any strategy will surely falter.

There are many definitions of culture, ranging from the ubiquitous 'the way things are done around here' to much more verbose and complex explanations. The issue with these definitions is that they become so abstract that they struggle to describe the breadth and depth of the levels in which culture resides. One long-standing model[24] views culture working at three levels:

- At an external level are the *artefacts* of the organisation – those aspects of the business that are clearly observable – for example, the office building, interior layout (open plan or partitioned offices) and dress codes.
- More abstract are the *espoused values* of the business. This introduces the notion that behaviours are key to enabling culture. It is also a reminder that values are different from norms. Norms are implicit rules and regulations about how we behave (and are therefore powerful regulators of conduct). Values are about how we aspire to behave. In many businesses, these are noble, if hackneyed, phrases around respect, honesty, integrity and so on. The key determinant of how effective these are as a cultural enabler is how well they are modelled each and every day by leaders across the business.
- The core layer is *underlying assumptions*. Over time, the shared beliefs of leaders become an implicit way of conducting businesses. In short, these are ways of working and behaving that are so ingrained that most employees do not recognise they exist. If an organisation truly seeks to change culture, then it is at this level that meaningful change must occur.

In a practical sense, remote working, accelerated by the pandemic, will have a lessening impact on corporate culture. This is because the artefacts of the corporate culture model are not visible to new hires. They will have missed the implicit clues that are provided by external artefacts such as office layout, décor and dress codes. Furthermore, they will have difficulty imbibing the implicit norms and values that are subconsciously communicated during in-person interaction but filtered heavily when interacting through Zoom, Teams or other interactive media. These issues represent a considerable stumbling block to those leaders seeking to create a culture that is competitively differentiated. Just how do they communicate and model desired behaviours where in-person interaction is minimised and where non-verbal communication cues become so much harder to decipher when using technology to interact? Furthermore, when faced with the growing impact of the gig economy, just how does an organisation seek to maintain a cohesive corporate culture with a transient workforce that may not willingly imbibe the prevailing norms and values that are the social glue that binds team members together?

Culture is stable over time and hard to change as it represents the accumulative learnings of all the team members over a period. This is important for two reasons: first, leaders like to see themselves as cultural leaders and shapers and, in one sense, they are. The guardians of the culture, however, are not the board members but those long-serving employees working in customer-facing roles. Marks & Spencer was, until recently, a leading light in UK retail. However, it has struggled to adapt and change to modern ways of working, and its clothing business has faced constant erosion of market share as online competitors have attracted business away. Its 2018 annual report[25] recognised candidly that 'behind most underperforming businesses there sits organisational failure and culture that has proved resistant to change. Our case is no exception.' The key to cultural change in Marks & Spencer lies not in worthy boardroom utterances but in accessing the hearts and minds of the serried ranks of long-serving employees across its extensive store network to live and breathe the new and desired behaviours. Cultures need to adapt as a function of organismal evolution. Leadership behaviours are the primary cultural embedding mechanisms. Put simply, it is about 'walking the talk' or 'do as I do.' Many leaders underestimate how their every behaviour and utterance are scrutinised by team members for clues that help them understand how to thrive in an organisation and thus reduce their anxieties around their survival in the business.

A further way of explaining corporate culture[26] is show in Figure 1.3.

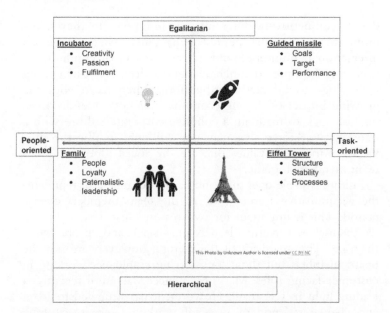

Figure 1.3 Four types of corporate culture
Source: Hampden-Turner, C. and Trompenaars, F., 2020. *Riding the Waves of Culture: Understanding Diversity in Global Business.* Hatchette UK.

The two axes are people versus task (horizontal) and egalitarian and hierarchical (vertical), which define four types of corporate culture:

- The **family** culture (people-oriented and hierarchical) is often run by a matriarch or patriarch who believes they understand what is best for the employees. At its best, this culture engenders much employee loyalty. Career progress is dependent on relationships with the owner, patriarch or matriarch. Current UK examples might include the Virgin empire and past Quaker-owned businesses such as Clarks and Cadbury.
- The **Eiffel Tower** culture (task-oriented and hierarchical) defines roles to ensure that key tasks are completed. The focus is on process and rigid structure that ensure that product is produced to quality criteria. Career progress is dependent on the acquisition of relevant job-related

knowledge and skills. Examples of these cultures might include German automobile manufacturing plants.

- The **guided missile** culture (task-oriented and egalitarian) is the predominant one in Anglo-Saxon cultures. The focus here is on forming teams to achieve strategic targets. It is the most performance-oriented of the four cultures. Career progress is achieved through merit. Examples of this culture might include General Electric, Ford and Dell.
- Finally, the **incubator** (people-oriented and egalitarian) is based on creativity and fulfilment in role. Team members think nothing of working long hours because they passionately believe in the concept or idea that they are developing. Career progress is achieved rather than ascribed. Internet start-up companies are one example of this culture.

This model enables two questions to be asked:

- the first is 'where is your culture now?', eliciting a conversation around this (NB: the outcome may be in more than one culture)
- the second is, 'where does your culture need to be to be fit for strategic purpose?', encouraging debate on this.

The answer to the second question should start to describe the behaviours that senior leaders need to enact to deliver the culture that enables the strategy. It should also illuminate the size of the gap that needs to be bridged for such a cultural shift to take place. It is comparatively easy to move vertically in this model (e.g., from Eiffel Tower to guided missile), harder to move laterally (e.g., from family to Eiffel Tower) and extremely hard to move diagonally (e.g., from family to guided missile). Note that this is not a cultural audit! Corporate culture is much too abstract a phenomenon to be strait-jacketed into a two-by-two matrix. But it does insert culture into the talent equation and gives a broad-brush means for constructive debate around a winning culture for the business.

For digital businesses, there is often a cultural tension between cultural continuity and digital transformation. Research[27] suggests that digital transformation without cultural continuity risks chaos, as the sense-making mechanisms of corporate culture are lost. Team members find themselves disoriented as their previous interpretations of the culture have been uprooted in the drive for digital transformation. Far better to deliver a digital transformation that contains elements of both cultural change and continuity. This allows digital transformation to progress (albeit at a slower pace) within a culture that team members both recognise and feel comfortable working within.

BUSINESS MODEL INNOVATION: THE LOGIC OF VALUE CREATION

In a similar way that corporate culture is an enabler of strategy, so business model innovation is an enabler of commercial performance. A business model can be defined as the way in which a business creates and captures value for a customer group. Value creation refers to how the business sustains competitive advantage over time and how quickly and effectively it can scale to meet demand. Digital business model thinking requires working through three dimensions (content, experience and platform) simultaneously to create a compelling customer value proposition, as shown in Figure 1.4.[28]

- Content refers to what is consumed. For some digital businesses, this can be wide-ranging, from digital products to more substantive physical products.
- Customer experience refers to all the touchpoints along the customer journey.
- The platform refers to the synchronised set of digital processes, data and infrastructure that deliver customer fulfilment. The key to this model is that this is not a linear process. All parts need to work in tandem with each other to deliver a coherent multi-product experience.

Technology by itself has no rational value. It only becomes useful when it is monetised by a business model. This is important, because the same technology funnelled through two different business models will deliver different commercial outcomes.[29] Business model innovation is not just the province

Content: what is consumed?	Information product	Product information, price and use details etc. Digital products, such as e-books, e-saver accounts, movies, software
Experience: how is it packaged?	Customer experience	Experience can include customer-facing digitized business processes, community and customer output, expertise for informed decision making, recommendations, tools and interface
Platform: how is it delivered?	Internal/external	Other business processes, customer data, technology; propriety hardware, public networks and partners

Figure 1.4 The three components of a digital business model
Source: Weill, P. and Woerner, S.L., 2013. Optimizing Your Digital Business Model. *MIT Sloan Management Review, 54(3)*, 71.

of digital enterprises. Manufacturing enterprises are also seeing the benefits of moving from product-to service-based revenues. This is termed servitisation and includes the addition of digital-based services and solutions as a complement to manufacturing offerings. There are two key benefits from this approach. First, it brings the business much closer to the customer and provides opportunities to develop relationships beyond the merely transactional. Second, as a result, it also a defence against being undercut by leaner and cheaper manufacturing competitors.

BUSINESS MODEL RENEWAL OR REPLICATION?

Some research[30] has identified four distinct types of business model innovation:

- fixation: with only minimal renewal or replication (such as energy supply companies or any number of public-sector institutions that always do what they have always done)
- replication: such as McDonald's – a global brand that has been operating the same business model since its inception in the last century
- renewal: such as Microsoft, which has transitioned from hardware product lines towards cloud- and subscription-based offers

- replication and renewal: it is this type that is of most interest, because research suggests that organisations that both replicate and renew perform better than those that just do one or the other and much better than those that focus on fixation; the notion here is that combining both current and proposed business models enables businesses to maximise their existing skills and capabilities while simultaneously addressing as yet unmet customer needs; one conclusion from research is that replication works well for the short to medium term, but that businesses that radically renew their business models perform better over the longer term

The implications of business model innovation for talent management are considerable. Leaders need to have the cognitive skills to spot early warning data (even if the figures read well) that the business model may be obsolete. The complexities of transforming business models require sound levels of general mental ability (GMA). Leaders will need to communicate fulsomely up, down and across the organisation to ensure that all understand the rationale for changing the business model and are committed to its effective implementation. Much of this is founded upon sound levels of emotional maturity – managing their own emotions and those of others in a calm and professional manner. They should foster a culture of creativity and innovation where team members feel comfortable sharing new ideas, where failure is positively encouraged and where learnings are shared widely across the business. Such skills place an enhanced emphasis on openness to experience, a 'Big Five' personality construct that is influenced by openness to imagination, openness to one's own feelings, openness to new ways of doing things and high levels of intellectual curiosity. Above all, it is about having a bench strength of talent who have the knowledge, skills and resilience to cope with the change and implement this right first time.

SUMMARY

The winners in the war for talent are those who will harness the benefits of AI, big data and people analytics to drive decisions. They will understand the semantic difference between digital disruption and transformation and tailor their strategies accordingly. They will have a clear digital strategy and will have developed the tactical plan to execute it. They will adapt their talent management practices to the realities of a post-pandemic world of work. They will embrace the gig economy as part of their talent pool. They will fully understand the critical role that culture plays in enabling the strategy and nurture and manage their culture accordingly. They will frequently review the relevance of their business model and seek to both replicate and renew to drive performance.

No business can survive without talented people within it. Thus, how talent is recruited, selected, retained and developed is core for delivering organisations' digital transformation. The next four chapters discuss these implications in greater detail.

THE BUSINESS CONTEXT. TEN TOP TIPS CHECKLIST

We understand the key semantic difference between disruptive technologies and sustaining innovation and have positioned our strategy accordingly	✓
We understand the trade-off between the aspirations of our business strategy and the probability of attracting the required talent to execute it	✓
We embrace data as a strategic asset. Our people analytic data are predictive and give us actionable insights that drive our talent decisions	✓
We understand where we are on our digital journey, the core technological capabilities that we need to develop and the leadership behaviours that will convert these into business transformation	✓
We embrace the ethical use of AI and we check rigorously to ensure that this enhances, rather than detracts from, our drive towards improved diversity and inclusion	✓
We understand where our culture is now and where it needs to be fit for strategic purpose	✓
All our leaders are aligned behind a key set of behaviours that will deliver the desired culture and are comfortable modelling these consistently in the business	✓

We have a clear talent philosophy that bridges the gap between our talent strategy and its implementation	✓
We embrace the wider definition of talent to include gig economy workers and we invest in them as we would our payroll staff	✓
We frequently review our business model – even if the business is performing well	✓

REFERENCES

1: Michaels, E., Handfield-Jones, H. & Axelrod, B., 2001. *The war for talent*. Harvard Business Press.

2: Joyce, W.F. & Slocum, J.W., 2012. Top management talent, strategic capabilities, and firm performance. *Organizational Dynamics*, 41(3), 183–193.

3: McCarthy, J., 2007. From here to human-level AI. *Artificial Intelligence*, 171 (18), 1174–1182.

4: Firth-Butterfield, K., 2021. Building an organisational approach to responsible AI. *MIT Sloan Management Review*. Available at https://sloanreview.mit.edu/article/building-an-organizational-approach-to-responsible-ai/. Accessed 10 March 2023.

5: Howard, A., 2021. Real talk. Intersectionality and AI. *MIT Sloan Management Review*. Available at https://sloanreview.mit.edu/article/real-talk-intersectionality-and-ai/. Accessed 10 March 2023.

6: Rogers, D., 2016. *The digital transformation playbook*. Columbia University Press.

7: Gartner, 2022. *Hiring trends for predictive analytics competencies in quality*, Quality Research Team, 16 June.

8: Dhillon, T. & Aurelio, D., 2021. FTSE 100 top and bottom performers over the last decade. Refinitiv data stream. Tajinder Dhillon. Available at https://lipperalpha.refinitiv.com/2020/01/ftse-100-decade-in-review/. Accessed 4 October 2021.

9: Christensen, C.M., 1997. *The innovator's dilemma: when new technologies cause great firms to fail*. Boston, MA: Harvard Business School Press.

10: Solis, B., 2017. The six stages of digital transformation. Available at www.briansolis.com/2017/01/definition-of-digital-transformation/. Accessed 10 July 2022.

11: Munir, K., 2021. Digital Disruption: Digital Transformation Strategies course. Judge Business School, Cambridge.

12: Howe, D.C., Chauhan, R.S., Soderberg, A.T. & Buckley, M.R., 2020. Paradigm shifts caused by the COVID-19 pandemic. *Organizational Dynamics*, 50(4), p. 100804.

13: Laker, B., 2021. Why companies should adopt a hub and spoke model post pandemic. *MIT Sloan Management Review*. Available at https://sloanreview.mit.edu/article/why-companies-should-adopt-a-hub-and-spoke-work-model-post-pandemic/. Accessed 7 October 2021.

14: Chung, H., Birkett, H., Forbes, S. & Seo, H., 2021. Covid-19, flexible working, and implications for gender equality in the United Kingdom. *Gender & Society*, 35(2), 218–232. doi:10.1177/08912432211001304

15: Altman, E.J., Kiron, D., Schwartz, J. & Jones, R., 2021. The future of work is through workforce ecosystems. *MIT Sloan Management Review*, 62(2), 1–4.

16. Porter, M.E., 1979. How competitive forces shape strategy. *Harvard Business Review*, 57(2), 137–145.

17: van Alstyne, M.W., Parker, G.G. & Choudary, S.P., 2016. Pipelines, platforms, and the new rules of strategy. *Harvard Business Review*, 94(4), 16.

18: Catlin, T., Scanlan, J. & Willmott, P., 2015. Raising your digital quotient. McKinsey & Co.

19: Westerman, G., Calmejane, C., Bonnet, D., Ferraris, P. & McAfee, A., November 2011. '*Digital Transformation: A Roadmap for Billion-Dollar Organisations.*' Cap Gemini Consulting and MIT Centre for Digital Businesses.

20: McCord, P., 2018. *Powerful: building a culture of freedom and responsibility*. Tom Rath.

21: Mensah, J.K., 2015. A "coalesced framework" of talent management and employee performance. *International Journal of Productivity and Performance Management*, 64(4), 544–566.

22: Ulrich, D. & Smallwood, N., 2012. What is talent? *Leader to Leader*, 2012 (63), 55–61.

23: Effron, M., 2020. What's your talent philosophy? The Talent Strategy Group. Available at https://talentstrategygroup.com/whats-your-talent-philosophy-the-original-article-observations-after-five-years/. Accessed 10 February 2021.

24: Schein, E.H., 2009. *The corporate culture survival guide* (Vol. 158). John Wiley.

25: Norman,A., 2018. Chairman's statement. Marks & Spencer Annual Report. Available at https://corporate.marksandspencer.com/annual--report2018/mands_annualreport_2018.pdf. Accessed 7 July 2022.

26: Hampden-Turner, C. & Trompenaars, F., 2020. *Riding the waves of culture: understanding diversity in global business*. Hachette UK.

27: Pedersen, C.L., 2022. Cracking the cultural code for successful digital transformation. *MIT Sloan Management Review*, 63(3), 1–4.

28: Weill, P. & Woerner, S.L., 2013. Optimizing your digital business model. *MIT Sloan Management Review*, 54(3), 71.

29: Chesbrough, H., 2010. Business model innovation: opportunities and barriers. *Long Range Planning*, 43(2–3), 354–363.

30: Volberda, H.W., Van Den Bosch, F.A. & Heij, K., 2018. *Reinventing business models: how firms cope with disruption*. Oxford University Press.

RECRUITMENT

INTRODUCTION

Recruitment is those activities that businesses undertake to generate job applicant pools, maintain and nurture viable applicants and encourage suitable candidates to join the business.[1] This chapter will discuss:

- defining a recruitment strategy
- the changing nature of the recruiter role
- recruitment marketing
- the impact of technology and social media on recruitment
- prioritising the candidate experience
- developing a compelling employee value proposition (EVP)
- volume recruitment and
- the challenge of recruiting digital talent

THE CHANGING NATURE OF THE JOB MARKET

Pre-pandemic research[2] suggested that people had become more restless. The number of active jobseekers grew by 36% over the four years from 2011 to 2015, and those termed super passives (i.e., completely satisfied and do not want to move) dwindled from 29% to just 13% over the same period. The same research also found a trend away from large organisations towards smaller businesses (defined as fewer than 500 employees). According to this research, the primary reason for changing jobs was for career advancement, followed by a

DOI: 10.4324/9781003349587-3

desire for more challenging work and improved compensation and benefits.

Post-pandemic research[3] has signalled some significant changes. The opportunity for flexible working now ranked second (behind wage or salary) as the most important reason to accept a role. Indeed, the importance of flexibility has displaced job location from its previous top five ranking.

The advice from this research is to listen to the individual needs of employees. For some people, going to a physical workplace is a part of their social identity and an opportunity to interact socially with others. For others, working from home leads to a much improved work–life balance.

THINK BEFORE RECRUITING

Recruitment should not become the default solution for enhancing talent in the business. Although new talent should bring with them knowledge and skills, there are other human resource initiatives that should be considered before embarking on a lengthy, expensive and potentially risky recruitment process – for example, job and organisational redesign, making better use of existing talent, reallocating work according to individuals' skills and preferences or redesigning work according to Agile principles.

Chapter Four shares a useful example (Ricoh Europe) of scanning internally for hard-to-fill talent, and there are also other ways in which current employees can help. One fruitful avenue lies in the power of referrals. Simply put, it takes one to know one, and it is frequently the case that talent will very often refer other great talent and introduce the recruitment team to alternative talent pools. As a result, new businesses have emerged to address this need. Real Links is an employee referral and internal mobility platform that seeks to generate referrals within the business through such techniques as a referral jam. HR selects the roles that it most needs to fill and invites selected employees to join for a half-hour jam where they compete for points and prizes through referring candidates for these roles in real time, using social media platforms.

It makes sound talent management sense to exhaust these different options before a decision to recruit externally is made.

RECRUITMENT STRATEGY

In a conceptual sense, strategic recruitment suggests that recruitment should be integrated horizontally with other human resource practices and integrated vertically with the overarching strategy of the firm. The interested reader is referred to models of this[4] that propose multilevel systems which describe how recruitment activities might be integrated into a complex layering of strategies, policies and practices, within a broader environmental and contextual framework.

In a practical sense, the prime objective of any strategy is doing things differently rather than just doing things better. Thus, it follows that businesses should seek to become competitively differentiated through the quality of their people, and that effective recruitment clearly lies at the heart of this. Effective organisations in recruitment undertake four key initiatives to deliver best-in-class talent to the business:[5]

- They have a strategy and a plan to execute it. They focus on what is important to the business. Thus, any recruitment strategy must dovetail with the organisation's plans, strategies and goals. Recruiters work with the business to deliver the right talent. Thus, it behoves recruiters to build relationships with line managers to ensure that they are actively involved in the process of strategy and are emotionally committed to making it work.
- They form a cross-functional working group to review the performance and aims of the process and make changes. In this way, the hiring process is constantly evolving and adapting to changing demands, both internal and external.
- They focus most attention, time and resource on those roles that are mission-critical and thus have the most commercial impact. Likewise, they understand that a scattergun approach to sourcing talent works less well than a tight focus via a few selected channels.
- Finally, they adopt an assertive approach to sourcing candidates for the role and to building a pipeline for the future. This has significant implications for the role of the recruiter, as shown in Table 2.1.

Table 2.1 Changing nature of the recruiter's role

Old	New
'Order taker' of line manager requests	Consultative business partner
Multi-source approach to selecting talent	Scanning data to select chosen channels
Posting the position	Researching and understanding the role
Reviewing and screening résumés/CVs	Market research and talent mapping
Phone screening candidates	Engaging with candidates
Interviewing and assessing	Interviewing, assessing and selling
Candidate offer	Closing the candidates
A slave to the process	A competitive will to win

Source: Adapted from Parkin, S., Leading practices in building a successful approach to talent acquisition, in Berger, L.A. and Berger, D.R., Eds., 2018. *The Talent Management Handbook: Making Culture a Competitive Advantage by Acquiring, Identifying, Developing, and Promoting the Best People*. New York: McGraw-Hill Education. Reproduced with kind permission from McGraw Hill.

Thus, this is part of a much wider trend away from regarding recruitment as an art form towards greater comfort with technology (social media and applicant tracking systems) and people analytics (as discussed in more detail in Chapter Four) driving a more data-driven approach to key recruitment decisions. This also suggests that recruiters who win in the war for talent need be self-driven, highly energetic, super-networked and suitably assertive to compete effectively in the hyper-growth environment for top talent predicted for the future. As such, there is a school of thought that suggests that talent acquisition needs to be taken out of the HR function, as it now requires fundamentally different skill sets. and this interesting viewpoint is debated further in Chapter Six.

RECRUITMENT MARKETING

Faced with tight labour markets and adverse demographic trends (declining numbers of entrants to the job market and impending retirement of older workers), recruiters have turned to marketing concepts to understand applicant decision making better. Brand equity research suggests that creating positive and favourable impressions in the minds of consumers enhances the probability that a brand will be chosen ahead of competitors' products. Researchers[6] recognised that these same thought processes might also influence potential applicant perceptions about which organisation to join, and that media publicity can influence recruitment activities. Others[7] have since built on this, identifying four early recruitment practice measures (publicity, sponsorship, word of mouth endorsements and advertising) and sought to measure how these might impact potential applicant perceptions. This has highlighted how complex candidate decision making can become, in this instance supporting a mediation model where early recruitment practices affect application decisions through their impact on employer brand image.

Thus, investment in a company's reputation is also a recruitment investment, if this attracts further candidates to apply, and forms part of the relatively new concept of recruitment marketing. Whereas traditional recruitment has been focused on specific, current or predicted hiring needs, recruitment marketing aims to promote the company as an appealing employer to facilitate future hiring. The further difference between traditional recruitment methods and current realities is that the choice of media is now much broader, encompassing social media such as blog posts, videos and online employee interviews.

This perspective impacts recruitment in several ways: for example, it places the potential applicant and candidate at the forefront of recruitment policies. This much broader conceptualisation encompasses perspectives that view product advertisement as an investment in recruitment and recruitment as brand promotion. In a practical sense, this works in a positive way, as potential candidates infer attributes of a company based on their customer interaction. For example, Virgin Atlantic's consumer advertising is frequently accompanied by an increase in cabin crew applications from those attracted to the brand and its distinctive culture. But it can also work in an adverse sense too. For example, in 2019, British Airways saw its corporate reputation slip to 55th out of 65 companies in its Airlines Reputation Index, which was a four-year low, after being hit by IT failures, a data breach and strike action by pilots.

More specifically, resourcing teams should seek to employ marketing techniques to attract the right talent to the business. Such techniques include 'personas' that are composite sketches of a desired market segment. These enable recruiters to target the right candidates with the right messages, through the right sourcing channels.

MOVING AWAY FROM GENERATIONAL STEREOTYPING

Such personas are part of a movement towards segmentation by behaviour rather than through more stereotypical segmentations. There has been a tendency to focus on the millennial and Gen Z generations (anyone born between 1981 and 1996 is considered a millennial, and anyone born from 1997 onward is part of Gen Z)[8] as a key segment of the talent market, as these are assumed to be digital natives. Whether such generational segmentations are helpful in forming talent management strategies is a moot point. This is because the fundamentals of what workers require from a role, noted in greater detail in Chapter Four (meaningful work, autonomy, competence and relatedness, underpinned by effective leadership), have not changed over the years. Marketers have used the idea of generational groups to segment consumers and target their advertising. HR practitioners have caught on to this idea and used it as an explanation for employee differences in attitudes and behaviours across the talent spectrum. However, there is a growing antipathy to the idea that people are fundamentally different depending on when they were born. Some research[9] noted that there is minimal empirical evidence to support the idea of generational differences, that there is much evidence of alternative explanations for differences and, finally, that there is little or no support for the efficacy of interventions designed to address these differences. Even more concerning, the same research suggested that the use of such stereotypical casting to segment the workforce could be discriminatory. In short, the science is unclear as to whether there are any significant differences regarding job-related attitudes between previous generations and millennials or Gen Z today.[10]

The data are clear – talent management should discard outdated and restrictive stereotyping in favour of broader-based, more cognitive and behavioural classifications that span the generations.

MOVING TOWARDS BEHAVIOURAL MARKETING

The focus is now much less on demographic information and much more on micro-segmentation targeting individual customers at a particular time based on behavioural prediction. Behavioural marketing sits at the summit of the recruitment funnel and helps businesses to engage with and nurture talent. It scrapes and gathers data from diverse sources (e.g., opening a job advertisement or visiting a career site) to predict when a candidate is ready to accept another role and thus can interact with the candidate on their career aspirations in a focused and meaningful way. In this way, recruiters can now track whom the role is attracting, the nature of content that potential applicants are attending to, and those attraction initiatives that are working and those that are not. In short, behavioural marketing automation produces data that help to track, measure and collate candidate preferences and behaviours to assess a candidate's readiness to move role.

THE IMPACT OF INFORMATION TECHNOLOGY ON RECRUITMENT

Without doubt, the arrival of the internet has been a significant disruptor in recruitment, with several traditional recruitment advertising companies folding to the benefit of nimbler-footed, technology-based competitors.

Internet recruitment uses internet-based technologies to develop relationships with potential candidates, build applicant pools, maintain and nurture viable clients and encourage candidates to join the company.[11] For some, this definition may be counter-intuitive. This is because it assumes that technological enhancement helps, rather than hinders, candidate relationship management. The reality is that recruiter time is now freed up to invest much more in developing relationships with potential candidates, and this is especially facilitated by the rise and usage of social media.

SOCIAL MEDIA

The idea of using social media to research likely candidates is now an accepted part of the hiring process. The advent of AI has enabled recruiters to tap into multiple social profiles and form judgements about their values, belief systems and personality traits; it also offers recruiters improved access to passive candidates and an opportunity to start relationship building.[12] The use of social media to inform on candidates' likely suitability for the role suggests that this may now become a psychometric measure. This is an interesting development as it broadens the concept of psychometric measurement beyond the confines of aptitude testing and personality measurement and is discussed further in Chapter Three, Selection.

As part of behavioural marketing, social media now also sit at the top of the recruitment funnel and are a core part of recruitment marketing. From the candidates' perspective, it allows them opportunities to assess the culture. Thus, it is vital that firms pay close attention to how their culture is communicated across all digital media. To echo comments in Chapter One, if firms do not manage their culture, others will manage it for them. To this degree, the entirety of a firm's digital footprint now forms a substantial and implicit part of its recruitment marketing.

There are some caveats. Some candidates may be blissfully unaware of AI's capability within the recruitment process. Just what is being measured, and how? Organisations need to be transparent about AI's full capability and communicate this to candidates in ways that positively reinforce, rather than negatively impact, the employer brand. This forms part of a much larger debate about ethical and legal factors across the spectrum of talent management. In 2018, Amazon abandoned its plans to develop a machine learning tool that would scan applicants' résumés and automate the search for talent because their system had taught itself that male candidates were preferable.[13] This suggests that, for an algorithm to be fair, it must be transparent, and, as will be discussed further in both this chapter and the next, such transparency is the Achilles heel of many digital recruitment and selection processes.

FACILITATING SELF-SELECTION

One of the aims of an effective recruitment strategy must be to allow unsuitable candidates to self-select out. Technology enables this, as illustrated by the Netflix culture and value statement (Seeking Excellence) on their website. There will have been people who were tempted to join Netflix at the outset but were deterred later, having scanned the website and understood the distinctive culture envisaged for the business. Self-selection is enhanced further by good aesthetics in website design and customised information. For example, person–organisation fit and other data that are personally relevant to jobseekers are based on information that they have wittingly (or unwittingly) supplied and that allows applicants with a poorer 'fit' to screen themselves out. This works in reverse too, with some research[14] linking customisation to high-quality applicant pools.

In a similar vein, internet recruitment has important benefits for diversity and inclusion. Those websites that depict racially diverse team members will increase attraction of those minorities to the organisation. This places a keen emphasis on how both the message and design of the website impact company recruitment processes, enhance potential candidate perceptions and implicitly encourage minority group members to self-select in.

PRIORITISING THE CANDIDATE EXPERIENCE

All of us have, at some time or another, been frustrated with technology that took too long to access and was too burden-some to navigate. The feelings that a candidate experiences influence their decision to apply to an organisation or accept a job offer. Recruiters will want their firm to stand out for the right reasons, and the candidate experience is critical to this.

Research[15] into 'Improving the candidate experience' suggests that those organisations who set out to foster greater candidate connectivity with their brand and who also deliver a high-quality candidate experience are much more likely to attract high-quality talent. The authors propose a three-factor conceptual framework (specifically for assessment processes, but just as relevant for recruitment) that signals positive organisational qualities. These include the need to:

- display informational fairness (transparency across the process signalling high-quality practices) and give candidates clear application instructions
- ensure social fairness (treating candidates in a warm and respectful manner signalling co-operative corporate behaviours) and thank candidates for their interest in the organisation
- foster uncertainty reduction (increasing feelings of candidate control, signalling the organisation's attention to both well-being and trust); for example, send a confirmation email when candidates have applied and send a rejection letter or offer to an interview quickly

CANDIDATE ACCEPTANCE OF NEW TECHNOLOGIES IN RECRUITMENT

There is an intuitive sense that the automation of recruitment dehumanises the application process for applicants seeking a relationship with a potential employer rather than a transactional online process. The referral jam platform described earlier reinforces the power of building community through social media. Researchers[16] have specifically studied the acceptability to candidates of video-enabled social media as a recruitment tool. The results indicated that, while privacy concerns did exist, if organisations were only using video-enabled social media as part of their e-recruitment strategy to be perceived as 'trendy,' then applicants were less likely to apply for the job. Candidates must perceive authenticity in the whole recruitment process. Just as in the conceptual framework above, there needs to be a 'give-and-take' philosophy behind e-recruitment strategies. Information and system quality are important determinants in predicting the success of the type of technology in use. Candidates much prefer a technology-mediated tool where feedback is formative (rather than summative) and immediate. Although technology has a key role to play in effective recruitment, it runs secondary to brand perception, which is still the key component of organisation attractiveness and highlights the importance of a compelling EVP.

DEVELOPING THE EMPLOYEE VALUE PROPOSITION

Why should a talented person come and work for you? Talented people have a choice. So, what is it about your organisation that makes it an especially compelling place to work? Netflix was clear that the development of its culture and its dissemination using social media had a profound effect in attracting people with the desired knowledge, skills and attitudes. Indeed, the Netflix Culture deck on YouTube has attracted over 17 million views. HubSpot has also used this medium to share its culture, with over 6 million views. Both businesses are clearly working to differentiate their culture from others as a key part of communicating their EVP.

The EVP is the sum of the perceptions and experiences that employees gain by working in a business. These vary in make-up. In the war for talent,[17] they comprise exciting work, opportunities for development, lifestyle, working for a great company, and wealth and rewards. Research by Gartner[18] suggests a hierarchy of attributes, with compensation, work–life balance and stability rated as the top three. Those businesses that hire talent on the back of a false or unsubstantiated EVP incur unnecessary hiring costs, as talented people sense the mismatch between the EVP expectations and stark realities. One measure that all is not well with the EVP is a spike in exits at around six months' tenure as disillusioned talent cut their losses and seek alternative employment.

This much is evidenced by the contrasting fortunes of PwC and Barclays Bank. PwC is a multinational professional services organisation, recognised by some[19] as a pioneer in EVP. Much more than most businesses, PwC lives its values around diversity and inclusion and highlights career development and the opportunity to do interesting work. Within this context, brand reputation and perception count for much. In 2020, Barclays Bank's Diversity and Inclusion report extolled the values amongst others of 'Respect' and 'Integrity', and yet its management has not fared well modelling these values. Senior leaders were acknowledged to have used derogatory and sexist language about Amanda Staveley (CEO of PCP Capital) [20], and, in 2021, its CEO, Jes Staley, unexpectedly resigned owing to perceived inconsistencies in his account of his relationship with Jeffrey Epstein, the disgraced financier [21]. The lesson here is that it really does not matter what the organisation's EVP is. If the behaviours of its senior leaders are exposed as inconsistent or outdated, then the die is cast, and talented people will look elsewhere.

There are any number of EVP models in the literature, but that shown in Figure 2.1[22] is a useful guide to steer those building their EVPs to ensure that they are competitively differentiated

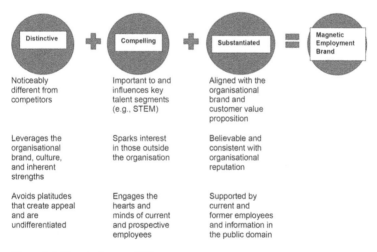

Figure 2.1 Developing an EVP
Source: Sorensen, A. & Pearce, A. Novel ways to win the battle for great talent in Berger, L.A., Berger, D.R. & Education, M.H. (Eds.), 2018. *The Talent Management Handbook*. McGraw-Hill Education. Reproduced by kind permission of McGraw-Hill.

(distinctive), relevant to key talent segments (compelling) and 'live' in the business (substantiated).

Building a compelling EVP should not be an expensive process driven by external resource. Rather, it should be derived internally and built bottom–up. Data should come mostly from employees, customers and key stakeholders and thus reflect the culture and values of the business, rather than a stylised idyll from the boardroom. One of the side benefits of this exercise is the opportunity to revisit the culture. How is this communicated externally? How accurate a representation is this, and just how distinctive and attractive is it? The success factors involved in creating a compelling EVP are well trailed elsewhere,[23] but it must align with the customer value proposition (talented people are customers before they become employees) and last throughout the employee life cycle, as social media platforms such as LinkedIn and Glassdoor are powerful opinion formers for those considering their next role. Most importantly, it is relational, not transactional. Put simply, a modern-day EVP is an 'ecosystem of support, recognition and values that an employer provides to employees to achieve their highest potential at work.'[24]

VOLUME RECRUITMENT

For many organisations, the recruitment of specific job roles is a continuous process. For example, hospitality companies are always seeking chefs, and IT companies continually recruit software engineers. This volume recruitment process may use applicant tracking systems (ATSs) that analyse, track and strategise talent acquisition processes. They can store and process vast volumes of data. Most will contain features that schedule interviews, distribute messages and customise the import and export of data. Some confuse ATSs with candidate relationship management (CRM) systems. In simplistic terms, an ATS is a workflow and compliance tool that manages applicants, whereas a CRM system is a candidate database that enables recruiters to nurture relationships with candidates prior to the application process, with the aim of creating a reservoir of talent to be tapped as the need arises. The aim here must be to fuse the two systems to capture the advantages of both an ATS (functional speed and efficiencies) and a CRM system (strong candidate relationships), to drive improved data-driven hiring decisions and, critically, to deliver an improved candidate experience.

One such solution is to embrace recruitment marketing automation. Not only does this recruitment software help companies to automate previous manual tasks – and thus speed up time to hire and reduce cost per hire – but its emerging technology employs advances in tracking technologies, machine learning and predictive analytics to both build and nurture talent pools to stay ahead of the demand for talent. The case study in Box 2.1 is one exemplar of how this system offers both candidates and recruiters enhanced data with which to make quicker and more robust hiring decisions.

BOX 2.1   CASE STUDY: CANDIDATE.ID

Candidate.ID, an iCIMS company, offers an inhouse recruitment tool that encompasses the benefits of both an ATS and a CRM system but takes these to another level through some unique features. In a holistic sense, it offers recruiters the opportunities to engage with their target population at scale and uses technology to deliver competitive advantage by engaging with talent who are already connecting with the brand. Candidate.ID uses AI-driven automation to track and score each candidate's interactions during the hiring process across numerous applications (e.g., job boards, websites and social media). Each time a candidate interacts with the pipeline, the automation software monitors this and continually updates its system offline to generate a candidate score that has now factored in 'motivation to move' with job-relevant knowledge, skills and abilities. Thus, recruiters now have a database of those 'cold,' 'warm' and 'ready now' candidates in real time.

In the past, recruiters have been skilled at generating large pools of applicants but less so at nurturing them. Candidate.ID gives time and control back to the recruiters, enabling them to invest in personalised conversations and long-term relationship building that can be leveraged for future roles to come.

EXECUTIVE SEARCH

At the other end of the recruitment spectrum lie executive search companies. These differ from other recruitment businesses because they work on a retained basis. As such, executive search consultants (also referred to as headhunters) 'search' or find candidates and invite them to interview. Thus, it makes sense to use executive search when the roles are at a senior level and where a fair degree of discretion is required, both to protect the client brand and also to connect suitable candidates with vacancies that they were not aware of or, indeed, actively looking for. Finally, executive search is relevant for those roles requiring a rare skill set or a particular knowledge domain. The executive search business faces two key challenges. First, unlike other professional services organisations, there are no professional qualifications required to set up a headhunting business. This inevitably means that there is a considerable degree of variance in performance across firms. Second, thus far, the industry has been largely immune to digital disruption. However, automation and advanced data analytics have now enabled some clients to move their search practices 'in house.' In a broader sense, this suggests that AI should be viewed by headhunters as an aid not a hindrance, and certainly never as a replacement for human insights, especially for high-stakes roles.

Those executive search firms who are clearly differentiated by a sector level of knowledge and expertise, who both foment and leverage long-standing advisory and consultative relationships and who operate in niche markets will be much less likely to be impacted by the unremitting march of digital disruption.

THE CHALLENGE IN RECRUITING DIGITAL TALENT

Recruiting talent across the globe is becoming harder, not easier. Even China, with a population of over 1.4bn, suffers from talent shortages, especially in digital talent. In 2020, Nancy Wang, head of talent solutions of LinkedIn China, noted that there

> are very few companies lacking strategies to hire more digital talent. The main reason is that companies cannot attract enough digital

talents in the market. All firms are competing for the same small pool of leading talents, such as data scientists and algorithm engineers.[25]

LinkedIn highlighted the top ten emerging skills in the Chinese talent market, including compliance, cloud computing, data science, small languages, risk management, interaction design, artificial intelligence, blockchain, digital marketing and full stack development. The point here is that a number of these skills were not apparent five years ago. Thus, the issue is just as much about the fast pace of change in digital knowledge and skills as it is about the quantity of digital talent available in the marketplace. Such shortages are repeated across the globe.

More practically, one avenue of attraction is to use technology-specific communities. For example, Slack is a business communication platform. Most chat on Slack happens in channels, and these can be both open and private. Thus, it makes sense to search where known talent lives and works. This provides networking opportunities to establish rapport and build connections that can be leveraged later.

As noted, attraction and assiduous networking form the first part of the recruitment process. The next is to offer a compelling remuneration and benefits package. Nowhere is the tech war hotter than in Silicon Valley. In 2021, Alphabet Inc., which owns Google, adopted a new cash bonus plan that allows the firm to give employees bonuses of almost any size for almost any reason. Six months later, in 2022, Amazon.com announced that it was doubling the cash it could now pay to employees in a year. As discussed in Chapter Four, money is rarely a satisfier, but it is a dissatisfier. People will be more open to leave if they feel that their pay is inequitable in some way. They may not necessarily work any harder if you pay them more.

Outside the recruitment hothouse of Silicon Valley, tech talent seeks flexible and remote working and learning and development opportunities. A survey of developers conducted by Stack Overflow[26] asked developers what drove them to look for a new job. Better compensation was by far the most common factor for respondents, with 70% of them noting that more pay was important. Wanting to work with innovative technologies was the second most popular factor. This is an important driver. In the survey, 75% of respondents noted that they learn an innovative technology at least every few months or once a year. This reinforces how quickly innovations happen and developers are constantly learning to keep their skills fresh and presents challenges to L&D professionals in ensuring timely and relevant learning.

Finally, hunting for tech talent should not be restricted to known hotspots. Employers can scale projects with talent from anywhere in the world who can help to fill short-term and project-based roles. This will inevitably aid access to a more diverse range of talent and reinforces the notion discussed in Chapter One that talent has a much broader definition than just those people on the company payroll. In a similar vein, recruiters and line managers must scour their organisation for internal talent – in short, 'grow your own' through developing existing employees with the knowledge and skills they need to transition and succeed in internal roles.

BLENDING FTE WITH THE GIG ECONOMY

At a strategic level, finding and retaining the right digital talent involve a complex alchemy ensuring that the interactions of purpose, people and processes are aligned with the organisational strategy and are flexible and responsive enough to adapt to changing market conditions. This is no mean feat and requires a significant rethink from more traditional models of hiring digital talent. One solution[27] is to blend two seemingly competing models of attracting talent, from skilled contractors and consultants on an on-demand basis and a core set of employees.

Chapter One noted the impact of the gig economy on talent management strategies, and, pre-pandemic, there had been significant growth of this talent pool across the western world. To recall, workers get paid for each 'gig' they do rather than receiving a regular wage. This attracts people who seek flexible hours as they balance their working lives with other priorities. Employers benefit from this as they do not have to pay employment costs unless there is work to do. This has not, however, been met with universal approval, with some civil liberties organisations and others lobbying the European Union to protect the rights of freelance workers.

The rise of the gig economy has been driven by online platforms such as Uber, Deliveroo, TaskRabbit and Upwork. Research[28] reports that the number of workers earning more than half their income from the gig economy varies nationally, accounting for just 1.6% of the adult population in the Netherlands (200,000 people) but rising to 5.1% in Italy (over 2 million people). As such, there is a blurring of the boundaries between gig economy workers and FTE. Selecting the optimal mix is frequently a function of the unique nature of the skills required to do the job and the time frames involved to complete the work. For example, freelance workers are frequently specialists in their area and can complete an immediate need without the heavier cost burden associated with full-time employment.

Thus, the work completed by gig economy workers is often complex and highly technical. Topcoder, for example, is a crowdsourcing business and the world's largest network of designers, developers and data scientists. It makes money through paying the wages of its community of digital experts and charging their clients accordingly. However, it transcends the traditional temporary recruitment model because its community is in great demand and has many organisations competing for its services. Thus, a firm's EVP needs to recognise this, and the winners in this war for talent will be those who are explicit about how they both treat and collaborate with contractors and the relationships that they wish to develop with them.

Companies that have been set up to provide contractors are now investing time and money in the development of their team to ensure that they have the relevant knowledge and skills. In this way, they are acting as much more than just temporary employment agencies. Employers are also investing much more in core employees. This starts with specific onboarding initiatives and is supported by learning and development interventions that go beyond just technical skills training to include, for example, project management skills and stretch assignments and secondments. More specifically, it may usefully involve more managerial skills such as how to lead teams of on-demand talent.

This requires HR leaders to step back and think in more integrative and holistic ways about how their work aligns with the group strategy and, critically, creates the enabling environment that allows digital talent to give of their best. As discussed in Chapter One, talent management processes that have been configured for traditional work environments are unlikely to be relevant for the digital age. Indeed, they may be unwittingly off-putting to the very talent segment that they wish to attract.

SUMMARY

The winners in recruiting will be those who welcome and embrace the relentless tide of digital disruption and think creatively about how recruitment marketing initiatives can build brand awareness and attract talented people. They will discard outdated stereotypical segmentations in favour of more behavioural and cognitive classifications. They will take time to build EVPs that signal clearly how the culture and values of their business differentiate them from competitors. They will think carefully about how to cast the net as wide as possible to encourage a diverse range of applicants. They will use applicant tracking tools and other software solutions to build relationships that freeze out competitors. They will treat candidates with care and respect, communicating frequently and transparently. They will strategise the optimal mix between employed talent and gig economy workers and build relationships with the latter that transcend the mere transactional. They will recognise that recruitment *is* marketing, and that recruiters need to be more informed, invasive, assertive and competitive than ever before to deliver the best talent to their business. In every sense, they will consider how emerging technologies can help them to recruit better, smarter and more cost-effectively, always remembering that talent is never a number but a human with choice.

RECRUITMENT: TEN TOP TIPS CHECKLIST

We have scanned alternative human resource solutions and determined recruitment as the optimal choice	✓
Every talent manager can clearly articulate the recruitment strategy and how this will deliver enough quality people to the business when it needs it	✓
Our recruitment strategy powers diversity and inclusion	✓
Every talent manager can clearly articulate the EVP and how this is both distinctive and compelling	✓
Every talent manager 'lives' the EVP in their everyday behaviours to ensure it is truly substantiated	✓
Our company has responsibly embraced social media as part of our recruitment marketing toolkit	✓
We keep candidates warm through frequent and timely information and respectful attitudes and foster trusting relationships that reduce their uncertainty across the recruitment process	✓
We deploy up-to-date talent acquisition systems with acknowledged algorithmic fairness	✓
We develop relationships with gig economy workers and businesses to ensure a consistent pipeline of talent for complex technical work	✓
Our recruiters are self motivated, highly energetic and assertive and deliver top talent to the business	✓

REFERENCES

1 : Dineen, B.R. & Soltis, S.N., 2011. Recruitment: a review of research and emerging directions, in Zedeck, S. (Ed.), *Handbook of industrial and organizational psychology* (Vol. 2, pp. 43–66). Washington, DC: American Psychological Association.

2 : LinkedIn Talent Solutions, 2015. Why and how people change jobs. Available at https://business.linkedin.com/content/dam/business/talent-solutions/global/en_us/job-switchers/PDF/job-switchers-global-report-english.pdf. Accessed 28 February 2022.

3 : Randstad, 2021. Attracting and retaining talent. Available at: www.randstad.co.uk/attracting-retaining-talent-2021/. Accessed 31 January 2022.

4 : Gully, S.M., Phillips, J.M. & Kim, M.S., 2014. Strategic recruitment: a multi-level perspective, in Yu, K.Y.T. & Cable, D.M. (Eds.), *The Oxford handbook of recruitment.* Oxford: Oxford University Press.

5 : Parkin, S., 2018. Leading practices in building a successful approach to talent acquisition, in Berger, L.A. & Berger, D.R. (Eds.), *The talent management handbook: making culture a competitive advantage by acquiring, identifying, developing, and promoting the best people.* New York: McGraw-Hill Education.

6 : Cable, D.M. & Turban, D.B., 2001. Establishing the dimensions, sources, and value of job seekers' employer knowledge during recruitment. *Research in Personnel and Human Resources Management,* 20, 115–164.

7 : Collins, C.J. & Stevens, C.K., 2002. The relationship between early recruitment-related activities and the application decisions of new labor-market entrants: a brand equity approach to recruitment. *Journal of Applied Psychology,* 87(6), 1121–1133.

8 : Dimock, M., 2019. Defining generations: where millennials end and Generation Z begins [online]. Pew Research Center. Available at www.pewresearch.org/fact-tank/2019/01/17/where-millennials-end-and-generation-z-begins/. Accessed 20 December 2020.

9 : Costanza, D.P. & Finkelstein, L.M., 2015. Generationally based differences in the workplace: is there a *there there? Industrial and Organizational Psychology,* 8(3), 308–323.

10 : Rotolo, C., Church, A., Adler, S., Smither, J., Colquitt, A., Shull, A., Paul, K. & Foster, G., 2018. Putting an end to bad talent management: a call to action for the field of industrial and organizational psychology. *Industrial and Organizational Psychology,* 11(2), 176–219.

11 : Dineen, B.R. & Allen, D.G., 2013. Internet recruiting 2.0: shifting paradigms, in *The Oxford handbook of recruitment* (pp. 382–401). Oxford: Oxford University Press.

12 : Brishti, J.K. & Javed, A., 2020. The viability of AI-based recruitment process: a systematic literature review. Available at www.diva-portal.org/smash/get/diva2:1442986/FULLTEXT01.pdf. Accessed 14 August 2022.

13 : Dastin, J., 2018. Amazon scraps secret AI learning tool that showed bias against women. Reuters. Available at www.reuters.com/article/us-amazon-com-jobs-automation-insight-idUSKCN1MK08G Accessed 21 February 2022.

14 : Dineen, B.R. & Noe, R.A., 2009. Effects of customization on application decisions and applicant pool characteristics in a web-based recruitment context. *Journal of Applied Psychology,* 94(1), 224–234.

15 : McCarthy, J.M., Bauer, T.N., Truxillo, D.M., Campion, M.C., Van Iddekinge, C. & Campion, M.A., 2018. Improving the candidate experience: tips for developing 'wise' organizational hiring interventions. *Organizational Dynamics,* 47, 147–154.

16 : van Esch, P. & Mente, M., 2018. Marketing video-enabled social media as part of your e-recruitment strategy: stop trying to be trendy. *Journal of Retailing and Consumer Services*, 44, 266–273.

17 : Michaels, E., Axelrod, B. & Handfield-Jones, H., 2009. *The war for talent.* Boston, MA: Harvard Business School Press.

18 : Gartner, n.d. Strengthen your employee value proposition. Available at www.gartner.com/en/human-resources/insights/employee-engagement-performance/employee-value-proposition. Accessed 2 January 2021.

19 : Recruiter.com, 2016. Top 10: companies that win employer branding. Available at recruiter.com. Accessed 14 January 2021.

20 : City A.M., Barclays' bailout talks peppered with sexist language, court hears. Available at www.cityam.com/barclays-bailout-talks-peppered-with-sexist-language-court-hears/. Accessed 15 May 2023.

21 : Duell, M. & Robinson, J, 2021. Barclays boss Jes Staley QUITS amid claims he played down his links to Jeffrey Epstein: Board says it is 'disappointed' over 'perceived inconsistencies' between what CEO said about relationship with paedophile financier and FCA investigation. Available at www.dailymail.co.uk/news/article-10151827/Barclays-Bank-boss-Jes-Staley-QUITS-ahead-Jeffrey-Epstein-report.html. Accessed 15 May 2023.

22 : Sorensen, A. & Pearce, A., 2018. Novel ways to win the battle for great talent, in Berger, L.A., Berger, D.R. & Education, M.H. (Eds.), *The talent management handbook*. McGraw-Hill Education.

23 : Jouany, V., 2020. Employee value proposition. the complete guide to building a great EVP. Available at https://blog.smarp.com/6-steps-to-build-your-employees-value-proposition. Accessed 14 January 2021.

24 : Greenberg, A., 2022. 12 examples of effective employee value propositions. Available at www.contractrecruiter.com/effective-employee-value-propositions/. Accessed 18 August 2022.

25 : Shijia, O., 2019. Talent shortage hampering digital transformation moves of firms, say experts. Available at Chinadaily.com.cn. Accessed 14 January 2021.

26 : Stack Overflow, 2020. Developer survey. Available at https://insights.stackoverflow.com/survey/2020. Accessed 25 February 2022.

27 : Kane, G.C., Palmer, D., Phillips, A.N. & Kiron, D., 2017. Winning the digital war for talent. *MIT Sloan Management Review*, 58(2).

28 : Huws, U., Spencer, N.H., Syrdal, D.S. & Holts, K., 2017. Work in the European gig economy. Available at https://feps-europe.eu/publication/561-work-in-the-european-gig-economy-employment-in-the-era-of-online-platforms/. Accessed 11 December 2020.

SELECTION

INTRODUCTION

Selection is the process by which organisations use one or more methods to gather relevant data from the assessment of individuals that help inform on their likely suitability for the role under review. This chapter will discuss:

- the changing nature of jobs required for the future
- the critical importance of a thorough job analysis
- a concise review of current selection methods
- the advantages and disadvantages of technology in volume selection
- the development of a digital competency set for high-stakes roles
- the emergence of selection techniques based on neuroscience with an accompanying case study
- a review of the impact of selection methods and processes upon fairness in selection

THE CHANGING NATURE OF JOBS

The digital revolution has led to a fundamental rethink of the knowledge and skills required for the future. At a national level, there is research[1] to suggest that automation creates more jobs than it destroys, with other research[2] suggesting that new digital companies create five times as many indirect jobs as direct jobs. This will deliver changes in all sectors, and it is the

DOI: 10.4324/9781003349587-4

changing roles in changing sectors which strongly suggest that new knowledge, skills and abilities (KSAs) are required to make this happen. This much is self-evident, because there are some job functions that only humans can do and skills that only humans can have – for example, jobs that require creative thinking and social skills.

The new skills required are both sector- and role-dependent but, in a holistic sense, it is intellectual skills that will be at the fore of new role requirements, especially complex problem-solving, process (critical thinking and process monitoring) and content (active listening, speaking and reading comprehension) skills. This does not signal the end of manual work but suggests that much of this will become more specialised. For example, there will still be a need for skilled workers to maintain and repair machinery, including robots. All this has significant implications for educational and training industries, with a pronounced focus on the training of IT skills and signalling a rebalance between vocational skills training and university education, with a renewed focus on the former over the latter.

START WITH THE JOB ANALYSIS

Any selection process must begin with a thorough job analysis. In the USA, the Equal Employment Opportunity Commission's (EEOC) Uniform Guidelines on Employee Selection Procedures[3] lay out the agency's standards for employment selection. They define a job analysis as 'a review of job information to determine measures of work behavior(s) or performance that are relevant to the job or group of jobs in question.' Competencies (clusters of effective behaviours) needed for the role are frequently used as a proxy for job analyses. For high-stakes managerial selection, the job analysis should consider the prevailing business context, strategy, culture and values of the business. For example, if a business is in financial trouble and in need of dramatic intervention, then falling back on pre-existing competency models is futile. Turnaround skills must come to the fore. In such instances, cultural fit is not useful if the existing culture is not fit for strategic purpose. In this case, the business likely requires 'cultural misfit' rather than 'cultural fit' – in short, someone to shape the culture rather than ape it. In this way, as noted in Chapter One, an analysis of the business context can dramatically alter the KSAs required for success in high-stakes roles.

EEOC guidelines note that job information is typically gathered by observing the job while it is being performed, interviewing or otherwise consulting workers who have done the job as subject matter experts or both. The 'measures of work behavior' – the standards that a worker needs to meet to do the job – should 'represent critical or important job duties, work behaviors or work outcomes as developed from the review of job information.' The guidelines warn employers to be vigilant about possible bias in the recording of job information and its analysis into measurements of work behaviour. 'All criterion measures and the methods for gathering data need to be examined for freedom from factors which would unfairly alter scores of members of any group.' Making sure that the measures are precisely keyed in is particularly important 'when there are significant differences in measures of job performance for different groups.' Within this context, job analysis is not just about gathering data to ensure predictive validity (see below) – it should also ensure equity and fairness.

SELECTION METHODS: WHAT WORKS WELL, LESS WELL AND NOT ALL

The measure used to assess the usefulness of selection techniques is called predictive validity – this is the ability to predict job performance and is usually expressed as a correlation co-efficient, where correlations run from +1.0 (a perfect positive correlation) to −1.0 (a perfect negative correlation). A test of general mental ability (GMA) has a high predictive validity and a low application cost. Put simply, across all roles, brighter people do better. A test of GMA and a structured interview offer the optimum cost-effective selection solution for most roles. The process of both transitioning towards and working within digital business involves much complexity. The more complex, fluid and dynamic the work environment, the more GMA matters. Some research[4] has indicated that the validity for GMA ranged from .39 for unskilled jobs to .74 for professional roles, suggesting that, for these latter roles, it may account for up to 55% of the variance in performance.

Some personality measures also predict performance. These measures are many and varied, but the science suggests that, for selection purposes, the Big Five personality factors (openness to experience, conscientiousness, extraversion, agreeableness and neuroticism) are the acknowledged gold standard model. Research has found positive links between some factors of the five-factor model of personality and measures of transformational leadership.[5] It had been thought that personality was largely immutable over time, but some research[6] suggests that the demands of a role can alter personality. Employees who experienced high workloads consistently over a 20-year period incurred developmental increases in extraversion, openness to experience and agreeableness. In short, they became more outgoing and assertive, more curious and more helpful and sympathetic. Those employees who had high job discretion did not incur similar developmental changes in personality. There are many and varied personality measures available on the market. Some require specialist training to administer and give feedback, and others need no training at all. Comparatively few are based on the five-factor model and have built-in psychometric properties that make them relevant and defensible as part of a selection process. For example, the Myers–Briggs Type Indicator is a popular measure but does not accord with these criteria and thus should not be used as a selection measure. It is a key ethical and commercial imperative to select with care the most apposite personality measure. Most industrial and organisational or occupational psychologists will advise when making this decision.

There are a wide variety of selection methods, and a detailed and comprehensive analysis of these is available elsewhere in the literature.[7] For most assessments, using composite selection tools works best.[8] Such assessment methods may form part of an assessment centre. These have been an established part of selection for external hiring, consideration of internal candidates for management roles, high-potential selection and employee retention in the face of workforce reductions. They involve multiple trained assessors observing, recording, classifying and evaluating assessees' behaviours considered key for effective performance in role across differing exercises. There are many useful books[9] that describe assessment centres in greater detail. In the past, these were physical events that occurred in an office or perhaps a hotel, but, increasingly, significant cost pressures have led firms to consider moving these online, and this trend will have been amplified by the pandemic. Research is scant on the utility of online assessment centres and their equivalence compared with in-person assessment centres. There will be advantages and disadvantages, one of the latter being that moving these assessments online will lessen the ability of the assessors to read and interpret non-verbal behaviour that forms a key part of group interaction. At the bottom of the predictive validity scale lie graphology and astrology. These are practically useless in predicting performance in role, and their deployment would likely constitute an unfair selection practice.

TECHNOLOGY IN VOLUME SELECTION: THE PROS AND THE CONS

The advent of globalisation and the internet has altered selection in many ways. It has had the benefit of bringing large numbers of applicants to employers. Sifting through these is inevitably resource-intensive, and one solution to this is to move selection online. The advances in technology, AI and machine learning have led to substantial growth of new forms of assessment such as gamification, digital interviews and the use of large data sets that have been gathered from diverse sources such as CVs and social media. Such new, technologically enhanced assessment processes offer clear advantages but also some equally clear and obvious disadvantages.

Chapter Two noted the increasing usage of social media as a selection tool. Recruiters are using social media to make selection choices, likely more for initial screening than final selection, but, nonetheless, social media now form part of the selection toolbox for many HR practitioners. Examples of social media include YouTube, Twitter, Facebook and LinkedIn. Research[10] suggests that social media are used as a secondary source of data to other more robust sources, but ease of availability and inexpensive access further suggest an increasing demand. The same research asserts that 93% of employers use social networking sites (SNSs) during their recruitment and selection processes. Some now use social networking information (SNI) to infer likely cultural fit and potential derailers. Indeed, 43% of employers in the UK stated that content found on social networking sites caused them not to hire a candidate.[11]

Thus, AI has an alluring appeal to recruiters and selectors as it provides a large amount of diverse data sets that help to sift through potential candidates. One emerging theory is that of talent signals.[12] As we access IT and digital applications, we leave behind a digital footprint of our interests and actions that can be used to infer behavioural preferences. Individually, such footprints do not amount to much, but AI has the potential to sift through multiple footprints very quickly and look across data to make predictions about human behaviour. Talent signals are disrupting existing selection processes. These forms of data are already out there in the digital domain, and businesses are springing up that aim to harness them for assessment purposes.

Assessing the utility of individual social media sites is complex because there are marked differences between them. LinkedIn, for example, is a professional networking site where information is primarily for job searches or the sharing of professional information. The data are publicly available to all subscribers. Facebook and other SNSs are mostly used for personal and social purposes. Research[13] suggests that using LinkedIn to assess personality traits produces only weak correlations. Facebook fares better in this respect, with slightly higher correlations. However, LinkedIn does deliver much less adverse impact on minority groups. Using LinkedIn to assess for cognitive ability produced only moderate validity. There is little surprise in this as making inferences of cognitive ability from academic achievements omits those who, in the author's experience, missed out on university education through maybe either familial or financial reasons, but who, when tested, recorded a higher level of cognitive ability than any number of their university-educated peers. The research concludes that using social media to assess for personality and cognitive ability is less effective than using more traditional measures.

As such, there is a significant divide between the creation and adoption of new technologies and the academic research to support them as valid, reliable and fair selection tools. This is a familiar refrain from industrial psychologists and the HR community and can be illustrated by the advent of HireVue, an end-to-end hiring platform business with a website that claims that its model 'no longer relies on CVs or assumptions. By standardising the interview process at scale with video, game-based and coding assessments, you can evaluate what truly matters.' The business has grown from 13,000 interviews in 2012 to over 20 million in 2021. A quick glance at the dates of the three references in Table 3.1 show research published in 2019 and 2021. In short, academic research on the utility of these new selection technologies lags their practical implementation by between five and seven years.

In a similar vein, practitioners should take care not to be seduced by slick sales talk that skates over sound theory and robust psychometric properties. For example, one gamification business trumpets that gamification 'is a massive success for candidates and employers,' citing impressive statistics on candidate attraction, decreased turnaround time and overall cost reduction. In short, it proposes financial outcomes but offers no statistical evidence that its selection technique enjoys robust psychometric properties (i.e., it measures what it is supposed to measure; is a reliable test or measure; does not wittingly or unwittingly discriminate against any minority group; and, critically, predicts future performance in role).

One of the problems with assessing utility is that companies with new technologies are reluctant to open their data to inspection by psychometricians and others who would seek to understand how these tests and measures have been compiled. Test publishers are not keen to do this, regarding their algorithms and other data as competitively sensitive information. This has the effect, however, of creating a 'black box' of data that some researchers now refer to as 'digital snake oil' – the unsupported mix of data and complex algorithmics unrelated to relevant psychological theory. The answer to this conundrum is for test publishers to make their theories, data and codes open source, allowing inspection by qualified professionals.

The ethical issues inherent in some new technologies are substantial, and privacy concerns abound. For instance, some employers have asked candidates for password access to their social media sites. In the USA, almost half of the states have passed laws prohibiting employers from asking applicants and employees for their social media login information.

That said, these new forms of assessment are here to stay. Practitioners should carefully balance the undoubted commercial and financial benefits with the dual imperatives of ensuring that their choice of selection tools complies with both regulatory (e.g., EEOC guidelines) and ethical requirements. Organisations need to carefully monitor applicants' reactions to new technologies, especially digital interviews. Some may be put off by the impersonal nature of these, but such negative reactions can be mediated by using organisation presentation videos before the digital interview starts. Increases in social interaction between the applicant and organisation members are associated with improved applicant reactions.[14] Moves to reduce assessment length come with a reliability warning. This is because reliability tends to increase as assessment length increases. When this happens, there are greater opportunities for random error score variability to cancel itself out. Thus, true score variation becomes a larger portion of the measurement, resulting in higher reliability. Table 3.1 summarises the pros and cons of online selection tools and technologies.

Table 3.1 Online technologies in volume selection: the advantages and disadvantages

Pros
✓ AI enables swift computation of multiple data sources (i.e., talent signals) that cannot be gathered, harnessed and analysed by other means
✓ Increased speed and low cost of administration and scoring are clear and obvious attractions for businesses that must manage large volumes of applications in a timely and cost-effective manner
✓ New technologies will provide a structured assessment process and allow for multiple evaluators to review and score the same recorded responses
✓ AI and machine learning algorithms should eliminate bias

Pros
✓ Applicants are attracted to organisations that use technologically current and engaging selection technologies
✓ Inclusivity is enhanced, as traditional approaches to selection cannot manage large groups of applicants

Cons
✓ There is an increased risk of applicants cheating if completing selection tests in remote, unsupervised settings
✓ There is a marked lack of supporting psychological theory for some predictors of job effectiveness (e.g., voice and facial recognition). For example, data from the US National Institute of Standards and Technology investigating facial recognition technology found that African American and Asian faces were misidentified 10–100 times more frequently than Caucasian faces[15]
✓ Similarly, studies suggest that six classic basic emotions do not correlate with their predicted facial signal[16]
✓ Technologies that use voice and facial recognition techniques at best dilute non-verbal communication, which forms a significant part of human interaction. For example, measurement of eye contact will inevitably be hard to measure during digital interviews if there is no one to make eye contact with!
✓ The empirical evidence to support validity, reliability and fairness is either unavailable or very hard to find
✓ Applicants reported higher perceived fairness when a human reviewed their CV than when a machine did[17]

MANAGERIAL SELECTION

CRYSTALLISED AND FLUID INTELLIGENCE

To recall, GMA is the best single predictor of performance in roles. There are two forms of intelligence.[18] The first is termed crystallised intelligence and measures the ability to compute with known data and skills that are accumulated throughout life. The second is fluid intelligence, which is the ability to work through new and novel data, make sense of ambiguity and make sound judgements under conditions of uncertainty, independent of acquired knowledge. Both are important for working through complex problems, but fluid intelligence assumes key importance for leaders working in highly strategic roles and in dynamic and fluid work environments.

For example, government leaders across the globe struggled to adopt a quick and effective response to the COVID-19 pandemic. There was little prior knowledge on which to base decisions. The scientists knew more than the politicians, but not enough to make definitive judgements. Thus, the situation called for high levels of fluid intelligence to make sense of the little that was known and plot a way forward. This type of scenario requires disciplined, critical thinking predicated on sound skills in logic, analysis and pattern recognition. Over time, as the knowledge base increases, what was fluid now becomes crystallised, and the decisions become more robust as they are predicated on sound, accumulated data. There are clear intellectual parallels with the digital world, which is fast moving and continually evolving and therefore requires superior levels of both intelligences to make sense of complexity and establish a competitive position.

DESIGN THINKING

Making sense of complexity places a premium on leaders' abilities to crunch key data quickly and efficiently in order to make sound judgements, especially under conditions of uncertainty. Design thinking[19] is an emerging problem-solving process that enables people to problem solve in the digital domain through a core set of three principles: having empathy with users, creating models through prototyping and showing a tolerance for failure.

- Empathy starts with putting the end user at the heart of the process through behavioural observation and inferences about what people really want. The key here is to use emotional language (e.g., want, feel and desire) to describe products. Such 'softer' qualitative data are just as important as 'harder' and more quantifiable data.
- Creating models through prototyping uses visual aids such as diagrams and sketches to make sense of complex data through pictorial representation. An example of just such

thinking might be the London Underground map designed by Harry Beck in 1931. It prioritises the pictorial representation of stations and lines and their interconnectivity over geographical accuracy. The creation of such resources is not prescriptive. Rather, they foment debate and challenge to communicate ideas.

- Tolerating failure: because the process of design thinking is iterative, there will be stumbles along the way. The Dyson vacuum cleaner had over 5000 iterations before the final model was approved. Thus, a culture of creativity and innovation within the team is core to enabling creative people to feel positive about contributing within a no-blame culture, where failing fast provides opportunities to learn quickly.

Design thinking is well suited to digital businesses struggling with complexity and looking for creative solutions to deliver value. End users want their interactions with technology to be simple, intuitive and pleasing. It is less relevant for stable businesses looking to improve operational efficiencies or working to timebound metrics.

TOWARDS A MANAGERIAL BENCHMARK IN DIGITAL BUSINESSES

Traditional managerial assessments have focused on behavioural competencies that closely resemble each other, differentiated only by the prevailing business context and acknowledgement of the perceived corporate culture and values. These do not, however, reflect the reality of working in digital businesses. To recall, Figure 1.2, 'What is your level of digital mastery?',[20] suggested that effective leaders of digital businesses are skilled in building digital capability (the 'what' of technology) and showing leadership capabilities (the 'how' of leading change). Both these skills need to be working in harmony to deliver digital transformation correctly, the first time. Leading change is the mechanism that converts technology into business transformation. Leaders of digital businesses set out a vision for the business, frame the way forward and allow competent team members to choose the means of delivery. They set out the culture for success and ensure that the building of digital capability across the business is fully resourced in terms of both technological sophistication and building a pipeline of digital talent. It is of critical importance to understand the opportune time to invest in digital transition. The decision to undertake digital transformation should be timed according to the readiness of the customers and not to follow commercial trends or as a sure-fire route towards commercial salvation.

DIGITAL COMPETENCIES

More specifically, the advance of digital transformation requires senior leaders to adopt new and different behaviours. Just adapting or changing what has been done before will not be effective. The digital agenda is transforming businesses, and senior leaders need to adopt a transformational change in behaviours in response. Table 3.2 describes seven core behaviours that all digital leaders need to show. These behaviours are based on research[21] that suggests digital transformation is changing the rules according to which businesses now operate, and senior leaders need to change their behaviours radically to make the most of the opportunities that digital change offers.

Table 3.2 Leadership competencies for the digital age

Competency	Old behaviours	New behaviours
Data analyses Core theme: converting data into a strategic asset	Data are collected and stored in a central analytics function	Leaders foment a data-driven culture across all the business
	Key data are held by senior leaders	Data democratisation leads to digital growth
	Data as a tool for optimising current business processes	Developing data to create long-term business value
Strategic thinking Core theme: competitive differentiation through platforms	Focusing on products	Focusing on platforms
	Adversarial approach to competitors	Co-operating with competitors (co-opetition)

Competency	Old behaviours	New behaviours
	Acceptant of a few dominant competitors	Leveraging the power of network effects to deliver winner takes all
Creativity and innovation Core theme: validating new ideas through rapid experimentation	Intuitive decision making	Continual use of A/B and multivariate testing
	Stopping at the first optimal solution	Developing minimum viable prototypes
	Failures to be avoided at all costs	Embracing failures as opportunities to learn
Customer focus Core theme: engage, empower and co-create with customer networks	Communications are a one-way transmission using mass marketing tools	Using technology to enhance two-way customer communication
	Customers are passive consumers	Leveraging how contented customers liaise together
	Marketing to influence purchase	Marketing to inspire brand loyalty and advocacy
People leadership Core theme: cultural leadership	Toe-in-the-water approach to digital transformation	Creating a technology-led business
	External hiring of digital skills to plug the knowledge gaps	Invests to enhance digital skills across the business
	Leverages existing people, skills and behaviours to drive incremental improvement	Fuses business and IT leaders' knowledge and skills to drive transformation together
Agile working Core theme: design of optimal work environments	Working within hierarchical organisational design	Working in small teams
	Delivering customer service through a complex mix of people and systems	Ensuring all have a clear line of sight to the ultimate user

Competency	Old behaviours	New behaviours
	Division of labour into functions	Fostering a culture of networked teams
Business model innovation Core theme: the logic of delivering business value	Views technology as sole enabler of business model innovation	Harnesses content, customer experience and platforms
	Current performance justifies persistence with the prevailing business model	Continually evaluates business model for relevance and utility
	Business model change is strategy-driven	Business model change is customer-driven

Source Adapted from Rogers, D., 2016. *The digital transformation playbook.* Columbia University Press.[21]

The key point here is that these behaviours are an 'and' not an 'either/or.' For example, past customer competencies might have stressed keeping closer to customers, building rapport quickly with key customer groups and developing and leveraging long-term relationships. These are still important skills, but now leaders need *also* to use platforms to foster two-way real-time communication with customers; use every opportunity to make the customer journey and experience as painless as possible; and access, engage, customise, connect, and collaborate with customers to become both a source of valued content and a focal point of customers' conversations.

Again, much the same can be said of business strategy. Michael Porter[22] noted the key difference between operational effectiveness (performing similar activities *better* than rivals perform them) and strategic positioning (performing *different* activities to rivals or performing similar activities in *different* ways). Thus, past competencies in strategic thinking would have focused on maintaining a keen external perspective, thinking broadly and holistically about how the business is competitively differentiated and how key political, economic, socio-cultural, technological, legal and environmental (PESTLE) issues might impact upon the business in the future. The core of these behaviours has not changed, but the focus of strategy is now *also* on how platform dynamics cut across traditional markets; strategy is now customer-driven because customer data are in real time. And, finally, the business leverages the benefits of digital working by disrupting through disintermediation (developing digital platforms that connect two sides of the market to remove the 'go-between').

These seven core behaviours are not exclusive. Assessors still need to measure other core managerial skills such as communication, influencing and relationship building, team working and delivery. The behavioural indicators for these have not changed. For example, senior leaders need to deliver, and to do this they must plan, organise, attend to detail, model and show total commitment to succeeding and achieving results. As such, whether the business is analogue or digital is largely irrelevant.

In a practical sense, these behaviours can be accessed best by structured interview techniques asking questions on each of the behaviours. For additional psychometric sophistication, assessors should calibrate the questions according to the business's stage on its digital journey. For instance, one would expect higher levels of digital competence from a developed FinTech business than from a business-to-business manufacturing conglomerate starting out on its digital journey, and the in-depth questioning and the quality and sophistication of the candidate response should reflect this. Therefore, one suggestion is that structured interview questions should be calibrated at three levels, dependent on whether the business is starting out on its digital journey (level one), some way there (level two) or setting the pace (level three).

Finally, some research[23] suggests that leaders need to critically evaluate themselves in readiness for the challenges of digital transformation not just in behavioural terms, as above, but also in rejecting outdated mindsets and adopting the new ones required to deliver a community of passionate and committed leaders to the business. For example, for leaders to deliver on data analyses, as in Table 3.2, they should adopt a 'digital savviness' mindset. Leaders need to be front and centre in conversations about the digital future and not sit above and abdicate responsibility to more digitally savvy others. In short, senior leaders need to be comfortable with their ABCs (AI, big data and cloud).

NEUROSCIENCE

Neuroscience is the scientific study of the nervous system and how it develops and works. Neuroscience analyses the biological and chemical processes that make the brain work. In short, it is brain science. New imaging tools and computer simulations can now offer further insights into the brain's anatomy and an improved understanding of how the brain, body and mind link up.

The tools that neuroscientists use include functional magnetic resonance imaging (fMRI), positron emission tomography (PET) and electroencephalography (EEG). As such, brain imaging now enjoys a robust scientific reputation.[24] In clinical settings, fMRI measures rooted in sound psychometrics, have the potential to become a powerful tool in neuroscience, allowing researchers to map the organisation of the average human brain and probe the brain bases of behaviours, from the simple to the complex.[25]

Neuroscience is an emerging tool in both the selection of top athletes and the development of military skills for the US Army. Research using neuroscientific approaches has already seen significant improvements in the development of rifleman skills, as discussed in more detail in Chapter Five. Consultancies are now adapting this science for the commercial world. Proponents of this believe that the next frontier for management lies in optimising leaders' brains as a source of competitive advantage.

Thus, neurocognitive assessments will deliver an analysis of each leader's brain and how it works. Each assessment process produces baselines against which progress (or regression) is measured. In this way, useful comparisons can be made with other high-performing leaders. These assessments can measure a variety of cognitive skills, such as reaction time speed, information processing abilities, stress responses, creative thinking and learning capacity. From a more developmental perspective, each subtest of the assessment produces data on the leader's specific brain functioning. From these data, experts can recommend a brain training programme to develop each cognitive function that is not performing optimally.

Recent research[26] has looked at ways of unifying personality theory with advances in neuroscience technologies. Academics have suggested that the Big Five personality trait theory has a foundation within the human brain as neural systems that constitute the neural equivalent of a personality trait. This research is in its infancy, and there are methodological problems with ensuring that proper research designs are used and taking due care in extrapolating experimental data from neuroscience research into the organisational sciences. The inevitable conclusion is that neuroscience is an emerging concept in the selection toolbox, as exemplified in the case study in Box 3.1.

The question therefore arises: will selection professionals be using fMRI technologies anytime soon? The answer in the short term is probably not. This is not because it has no long-term potential to predict performance, but more because neuroscience is an emerging science. As the case study shows, there are other, simpler ways of accessing brain functioning to make behavioural predictions.

BOX 3.1   CASE STUDY: ANZ AND PYMETRICS

ANZ is a global banking business with 10 million customers and 40,000 employees worldwide. The business seeks global consistency and standardisation across its selection processes. It recruits across graduate, high entry volume and gig economy roles. The bank retained pymetrics to develop customised selection processes across these three groups. The aim of the graduate process was to build adaptive graduates by supporting them to develop the critical capabilities ANZ requires to succeed in a fast-paced digital world.

Pymetrics (now owned by Harver) is a consultancy that uses gamified neuroscience to measure 90 cognitive, social and emotional traits of candidates. It uses concurrent validity studies (e.g., running its mini games on no fewer than 50 of the client's top performers) to identify data and trends for effective performance and likely fit. These data points feed into bias-tested custom success models. Candidates are invited to play the pymetrics games. From these, a recommendation on fit-for-role is made based on their gameplay and assessed against the success model. Interestingly, the prediction algorithm does not use any demographic data (e.g., race, ethnicity or gender) to assess for selection.

For its 2019 graduate campaign, ANZ reported improved:

- measures in the candidate hiring experience
- measures of fairness and diversity
- increase in applications
- screening-out time and processes
- reductions in recruiters' screening time
- acceptance rates of qualified candidates
- reductions in time to hire

To be clear, pymetrics is not using fMRI technologies to deliver this assessment. Rather, it uses its talent matching platform to capture behavioural data that, when integrated with human-centred AI and ethical design, enable workforce decisions. There are three key learning points from this case study. First, stakeholder engagement is key to ensure client commitment across the process. Next, there must be clarity about the advantages from a candidate and employee perspective. Finally, and in line with most businesses seeking to address the challenge of digital working, the selection process is dynamic, and the priority is thus to test, learn and adapt.

There are critics[27] of the neuroscience approach who note that, although advances in neuroscience allow one to understand better what is happening, they do not shed much light on why it is happening. In addition, and unsurprisingly, there are large ethical issues with the application and interpretation of neuroscience that need to be clearly understood. This has spawned the area of neuroethics, which relates to the ethics of neuroscience, and the initiatives undertaken to join up neuroethics with neuroscience.[28] There are others[29][,][30] who assert that some current tools of selection (e.g., self-report personality measures) have had their day, and that the future lies much more in neuroscientific approaches.

Neuroscience offers an interesting development in selection. One key practitioner lesson is that HR professionals and others should not be unnecessarily put off by the semantic notion of 'neuroscience' or its associations with notions of brain localisation hypotheses.[31] Neuroscience is here to stay but, like any other emerging technology, needs to be subject to the same levels of scientific rigour as other more established selection methods.

DIVERSITY AND INCLUSION

During the pandemic, there was a renewed interest in how businesses work to increase representation of women and minority groups. There are challenges in ensuring that selection systems are fair, and the EEOC states a vision of 'Respectful and inclusive workplaces with equal employment opportunity for all.' The EEOC has mandated federal laws that 'make it illegal to discriminate against a job applicant or an employee because of the person's race, colour, religion, sex (including pregnancy, transgender status, and sexual orientation), national origin, age (40 or older), disability or genetic information.' The penalties associated with infraction of these are swingeing in both financial and reputational terms. There are clear and obvious implications for the selection of employees, whether these be external hires into the business or internal selection for promotion, access to training courses or other talent management initiatives (such as high-potential programmes).

There are very clear social justice reasons to accord with both the spirit and the letter of the law in areas of diversity and inclusion. But there are challenges too. For example, intellectual ability is the best single predictor of performance at work. There is considerable debate about differences in intelligence across a number of diversity variables. The key point to remember is that IQ is only a predictor up to a point, usually at around 120. Over and above that, there is little incremental benefit in performance. This does mean that the cut-off points for cognitive reasoning tests need to be set at a level that the role demands. If a role does not need above-average intelligence, then the cut-off point should reflect that. For example, a role profile of a sales director role may focus more on relationship building, communication, persistence and influencing skills than high-level cognitive abilities. This further promotes a thorough understanding of the role under review before any assessment process can take place. EEOC guidelines support this, noting that tests should be job-related and consistent with business necessity and properly validated for the purposes for which they are used. This places a strong premium on measuring the right attitudes and behaviours with the appropriate tests and measures and clearly documenting the trail of decision making as part of the job analysis process described earlier in this chapter.

Adverse impact refers to the negative effect an unfair and biased selection procedure has on a minority group and has been measured statistically using the four-fifths rule. This is a rule of thumb that, through common use, has become an accepted standard, although both analyses and interpretation need to be tempered with a degree of caution. Research[32] suggests that adding tests of statistical significance to the four-fifths rule reduces false positive readings of adverse impact. Personality measures offer much less probability of adverse impact than cognitive measures, but they are significantly less predictive. This is the dilemma confronting recruiters and selectors as they seek to balance validity with fairness. There are several research articles in this area that offer useful practical tips on how to balance diversity and validity[33] and how using alternative and emerging selection technologies, such as situational judgement tests, can offer more promising solutions.[34]

SUMMARY

Effective selection professionals will conduct and log thorough job analyses to identify the knowledge, skills and attitudes required to deliver roles for the future. They will carefully choose psychometric tools to measure aptitude and personality that are transparent in demonstrating their psychometric properties of validity, reliability and fairness. They understand that a test of GMA combined with a structured interview represents a cost-effective and time-efficient selection solution for most roles. They will keep a keen eye on emerging selection developments (such as talent signals and neuroscience) while being mindful to ensure that new technologies offer validated incremental benefit over more established selection methods and tools. They will ensure that high-stakes roles for emerging and current digital businesses measure those behaviours that are specifically relevant to the digital domain. Finally, and critically, they will deliver assessment processes that are fair and seen to be fair and thus accord with both the spirit and the letter of EEOC guidelines.

SELECTION: TEN TOP TIPS CHECKLIST

We conduct and document a rigorous job analysis process to ensure that we measure those KSAs required for effective performance now and in the future	✓
From this job analysis, we select the most appropriate tools to inform the selection decision, balancing predictive validity with fairness	✓
We can measure crystallised intelligence, fluid intelligence and design thinking capability	✓
We use cognitive ability tests to measure GMA and thus enhance the predictive validity of our selection processes	✓
We only use measures of personality that are validated for selection purposes	✓
All that glitters is not selection gold. We let the science guide our choice of assessment tools	✓
We embrace technologically driven solutions for the selection of volume hires that are transparent about their psychometric properties and selection algorithms	✓
For high-stakes selection, we supplement our job analyses with a clear understanding of the strategy, culture, values and prevailing business context for the role	✓
We understand the behavioural changes required to deliver digital ways of working and we measure these using structured interview techniques	✓
All our selection processes are job-related, legally defensible and fair	✓

REFERENCES

1: Zobrist, L. & Brandes, D., 2017. What key competencies are needed in the digital age? The impact of automation on employees, companies and education. Deloitte.

2: Moretti, E., 2010. Local multipliers. *American Economic Review*, 100(2), 373–377.

3: Fritz, S. and Kleiner, B.H., 2000. EEOC guidelines that employers should know. Equal Opportunities International.

4: Hunter, J.E., Schmidt, F.L. and Le, H., 2006. Implications of direct and indirect range restriction for meta-analysis methods and findings. *Journal of Applied Psychology*, 91(3), 594.

5: Judge, T.A. & Bono, J.E., 2000. Five-factor model of personality and transformational leadership. *Journal of Applied Psychology*, 85(5), 751.

6: Holman, D.J. & Hughes, D.J., 2021. Transactions between Big-5 personality traits and job characteristics across 20 years. *Journal of Occupational and Organizational Psychology*, 94(3), 762–788.

7: Cascio, W.F. & Aguinis, H., 2018. *Applied psychology in talent management*. Sage.

8: Hattrup, K., 2012. Using composite predictors in personnel selection. *The Oxford handbook of personnel assessment and selection* (pp. 297–319). Oxford University Press.

9: Woodruffe, C., 2000. *Development and assessment centres: identifying and assessing competence*. CIPD.

10: Hosain, S., Manzurul Arefin, A.H.M. & Hossin, M., 2020. E-recruitment: a social media perspective. *Asian Journal of Economics, Business and Accounting*, 16(4), 51–62.

11: Grasz, J., 2009. Careerbuilder.co.uk. Available at www.careerbuilder.co.uk/uk/share/aboutus/pressreleasesdetail.aspx?id=pr28&sd=1%2f13%2f2010&ed=12%2f31%2f2010. Accessed 5 September 2022.

12: Chamorro-Premuzic, T., Winsborough, D., Sherman, R.A. & Hogan, R., 2016. New talent signals: shiny new objects or a brave new world? *Industrial and Organizational Psychology*, 9(3), 621–640.

13: Roulin, N. & Stronach, R., 2022. LinkedIn-based assessments of applicant personality, cognitive ability, and likelihood of organizational citizenship behaviors: comparing self-, other-, and language-based automated ratings. *International Journal of Selection and Assessment*, 30(4), 503–525.

14: Potosky, D., 2008. A conceptual framework for the role of the administration medium in the personnel assessment process. Academy of Management Review, 33, 629–648.

15: Singer, N. & Metz, C., 2019. Many facial-recognition systems are biased, says U.S. study. *New York Times*. Available at www.nytimes.com/2019/12/19/technology/facial-recognition-bias.html. Accessed 5 January 2022.

16: Durán, J.I. & Fernández-Dols, J.M., 2021. Do emotions result in their predicted facial expressions? A meta-analysis of studies on the co-occurrence of expression and emotion. *Emotion*, 21(7), 1550.

17: Noble, S.M., Foster, L.L. & Craig, S.B., 2021. The procedural and interpersonal justice of automated application and resume screening. *International Journal of Selection and Assessment*, 29(2), 139–153.

18: Cattell, R.B., 1963. Theory of fluid and crystallized intelligence: a critical experiment. *Journal of Educational Psychology*, 54(1), 1–22.

19: Kolko, J., 2015. Design thinking comes of age. *Harvard Business Review*. Available at https://hbr.org/2015/09/design-thinking-comes-of-age. Accessed 12 March 2023.

20: Westerman, G., Calmejane, C., Bonnet, D., Ferraris, P. & McAfee, A., November 2011. *'Digital Transformation: A Roadmap for Billion-Dollar Organisations.'* Cap Gemini Consulting and MIT Centre for Digital Businesses.

21: Rogers, D., 2016. *The digital transformation playbook* (pp. 1–18). Columbia University Press.

22: Porter, M., 1996. What is strategy? *Harvard Business Review*, November–December, 61–78.

23: Ready, D., Cohen, C., Kiron, D. & Pring, B., 2020. The new leadership playbook for the digital age. Reimagining what it takes to lead. *MIT Sloan Management Review*, 97(1), 1–19.

24: Jack, A.I., Rochford, K.C., Friedman, J.P., Passarelli, A.M. and Boyatzis, R. E., 2019. Pitfalls in organizational neuroscience: a critical review and suggestions for future research. *Organizational Research Methods*, 22(1), 421–458.

25: Elliott, M.L., Knodt, A.R. & Hariri, A.R., 2021. Striving toward translation: strategies for reliable fMRI measurement. *Trends in Cognitive Sciences*, 25(9), 776–787.

26: Hilger, K. & Markett, S., 2021. Personality network neuroscience: promises and challenges on the way towards a unifying framework of individual variability. *Network Neuroscience*, 5(3), 631–645.

27: Rotolo, C.T., Church, A.H., Adler, S., Smither, J.W., Colquitt, A.L., Shull, A.C., Paul, K.B. & Foster, G., 2018. Putting an end to bad talent management: a call to action for the field of industrial and organizational psychology. *Industrial and Organizational Psychology*, 11(2), 176–219.

28: Ramos, K.M., Grady, C., Greely, H.T., Chiong, W., Eberwine, J., Farahany, N.A., Johnson, L.S.M., Hyman, B.T., Hyman, S.E., Rommelfanger, K.S., Serrano, E.E., Churchill, J.D., Gordon, J.A. & Koroshetz, W.J., 2019. The NIH BRAIN initiative: integrating neuroethics and neuroscience. *Neuron*, 101(3), 394–398.

29: Barrett, P., 2020. Using self-report personality questionnaires for high stakes employee assessment. The end of an era? Cognadev. Available at www.cognadev.com/blog_100.html Accessed 13 November 2022.

30 Barrett, P., 2021. Which is better, Hogan or Cognadev? Cognadev. Available at www.cognadev.com/blog_115.html. Accessed 13 November 2022.

31: Diekmann, J., König, C.J. & Alles, J., 2015. The role of neuroscience information in choosing a personality test: not as seductive as expected. *International Journal of Selection and Assessment*, 23(2), 99–108.

32: Roth, P.L., Bobko, P. & Switzer III, F.S., 2006. Modeling the behavior of the 4/5ths rule for determining adverse impact: reasons for caution. *Journal of Applied Psychology*, 91(3), 507.

33: Ployhart, R.E. & Holtz, B.C., 2008. The diversity–validity dilemma: strategies for reducing racioethnic and sex subgroup differences and adverse impact in selection. *Personnel Psychology*, 61(1), 153–172.

34: Juster, F.R., Baum, R.C., Zou, C., Risucci, D., Ly, A., Reiter, H., Miller, D.D. & Dore, K.L., 2019. Addressing the diversity–validity dilemma using situational judgment tests. *Academic Medicine*, 94(8), 1197–1203.

4

RETENTION

INTRODUCTION

If the retention of talent was not a core management objective before the pandemic, it is now. This is because it has changed attitudes to working environments, with many workers enjoying new-found freedoms in how and when they complete their tasks and many who are now unwilling to surrender these as businesses emerge from the pandemic. Some employees will value their return to the office and the social and commercial benefits this brings; others will prefer remote working as their default option. As in any change event, communicating consistently through multiple channels that include one-to-one, in-person dialogue is key in garnering commitment. In this way, all will feel consulted and involved in changes to their role and work environment.

Media coverage of the 'Great Resignation' started in the USA, and there is some evidence of similar behaviours in the UK. A recent report[1] by Randstad UK quoted that 48% of respondents had switched roles in 2021, and that a competitive salary is still the main reason an employee will choose to remain in role (21%), closely followed by work–life balance (17%) and career opportunities (16%). As noted in Chapter Two, the opportunity for flexible working ranked as the second most important factor in deciding whether or not to accept a new role. There is a disconnect between the employee who values flexible working practices and a growing number of leaders who now want their employees back in the workplace. While

DOI: 10.4324/9781003349587-5

unemployment remains low, the employees will hold the upper hand. This power balance will shift if a recession looms, unemployment starts to rise, and employers lay off workers.

These data place a growing emphasis on how senior leaders can retain talent in the face of competitive labour markets and differing employee expectations. Whether this social shift in work–life balance is a temporary knee jerk reaction to the changing nature of work fuelled by the joint forces of increased digitisation and the pandemic, or part of a much deeper and long-term trend away from organisational life, is still to be understood. What is clear is that high-potential talent has a choice and, if not nurtured and developed, will be more open to headhunters' calls than talent in businesses with joined-up talent management initiatives. Within this context, this chapter will:

- briefly explore the concept of employee engagement
- understand motivation at work at individual, team, and organisation levels
- explore emerging developments in performance management
- summarise research in digital talent retention

EMPLOYEE ENGAGEMENT

Since 2019, in the UK there has been a statutory obligation for directors of large and medium-sized businesses to report on the arrangements relating to employee engagement and pay. Much of this is process-driven rather than about engaging hearts and minds. Some definitions of employee engagement conflate this concept with work engagement, which is commonly characterised by vigour towards work, dedication to work and absorption in work activity.[2] While this would seem to be a useful starting point, other research has grouped employee engagement into further categories such as a psychological state or an employment relations practice. And therein lies the rub – there is no one agreed definition of employee engagement. Indeed, one study[3] found that there were over 50 differing definitions of this concept. Thus, measuring this concept becomes complex, and, without a reliable measuring tool, it is hard to assess its organisational utility. The interested reader is referred to the relevant CIPD paper[4] which provides a useful synthesis of definitions, measurements and outcomes.

Rather than navel gaze regarding such an amorphous construct, a more purposeful approach is to review the psychological determinants of retention. Put simply, what psychological factors influence an employee's decision to remain in or leave a business?

MOTIVATION AT WORK

Creating a motivational environment where people feel empowered to give of their best will help to retain people in the business. For their part, businesses seek team members who are active and engaged (rather than passive and apathetic) and who are motivated to achieve. The question now arises as to how this goal is attained. The response is addressed at individual, team and organisation levels.

CREATING A MOTIVATIONAL ENVIRONMENT: INDIVIDUAL LEVEL

Self-determination theory[5] is a concept that arose in the 1970s and is now widely respected as a robust theory of motivation. It starts with the premise that people at work have three basic psychological needs that, when fulfilled, facilitate psychological growth and well-being:

- autonomy: people like to feel self-directed and in control of their own work environment and behaviours
- competence: people want to be proficient in their work and develop mastery over task activities
- social interaction: people have strong social needs and seek to both interact with and share meaningful experiences with others

These matter because they influence two forms of motivation. The first of these is termed intrinsic motivation and is the tendency to undertake a task because it is intensely enjoyable or interesting. This contrasts with extrinsic motivation, which is the motivation to complete a task because it gives a tangible reward contingent on performance. Intrinsic motivation is enhanced when accompanied by feelings of competence, autonomy and social interaction. The key learning here is to design roles around these basic needs and to develop line managers to encourage and develop them. This latter point is not as easy as it may sound. Some line managers may not be motivated themselves or have the skill set to do this well. This point will be discussed further across this chapter.

It is easy to view intrinsic motivation as a positive state of mind and extrinsic motivation as a negative one. This, however, is too simplistic. This is because there will be tasks at work that are not intrinsically interesting but need to be done. One approach is to encourage team members to internalise regulations so that they become self-determined. In this way, although the behaviour is proscribed by an external outcome or sanction, it has now become volitional or valued. Thus, leaders should find a meaningful rationale for an unpleasant task or behaviour. A useful example would be the uptake of the EU directive on GDPR. Initial compliance with this law entailed much bureaucratic activity that will have hindered normal work progress in most businesses. Most team members progressed this because they had recognised and internalised that non-compliance risked significant sanctions, both financial and reputational, and that adherence to this was valued by others to whom they felt both supportive and connected.

Although much of the research on motivation comes from an educational setting, the parallels with business are clear. To enhance intrinsic motivation, hire competent people (or develop them to achieve competence), give them control of the means of delivery and foster team working to satisfy their need for social interaction.

CREATING A MOTIVATIONAL ENVIRONMENT: TEAM LEVEL

LINE MANAGER LEADERSHIP

The line manager's behaviour and the team culture they foment are key determinants of a team member's work experience.

Every leader is a talent manager. They are responsible for the team, for its selection and development and retention. Theories of effective leadership abound, but, whether working in an analogue or a digital business or leading a multinational corporation, a hospital ward or a military platoon, the same basics apply: effective leaders set out clear directions for the team to follow, they are in touch with the social and emotional needs of their followers and they work with and through these to motivate them towards extraordinary performance. In practical terms, this means, among other things, catching people doing things right, giving frequent constructive feedback and seeking out opportunities to praise and reward liberally but appropriately. This is the basis for transformational leadership, as distinct from transactional leadership (where team members execute the work required to generate rewards). This may also include sanctions if there are obvious deviations from targeted performance. The parallels to the theories of intrinsic and extrinsic motivation are clear. And, like those theories, it is not an 'either/or.' Leaders need to apply both transactional and transformational behaviours to be effective in role.[6]

They should also create environments in which effective team working can flourish. Just because a leader has hired good people is not an indication that the group will perform well as a team. Team leaders should allow time for both team building and team working events that foster a collective sense of well-being and team morale. This is best achieved through participative leadership. This will improve the quality of decision making as team members contribute knowledge or data that the leader lacks. Moreover, the opportunity for team members to contribute to a decision usually enhances their commitment to executing it. Developing leaders at all levels to improve their leadership skills will reap retention rewards.

AGILE AND DevOps

AGILE

Businesses undertaking their digital journey need new ways of structuring and delivering their work. Agile working is a popular form of work redesign that emerged at the turn of the century as software developers realised that the traditional hierarchical ways of working were not fit for the digital age. Pioneers in the Agile movement worked to a set of behavioural values as shown in the Table 4.1. Again, the case is not that the factors on the left of the model are worthless, but that the behaviours on the right are valued more.[7]

Agile working[7] has three core elements:

- The law of the small team suggests that work is best done by self-managed teams, working effectively across functions on small, meaningful projects with direct feedback from the customer. This links to the theory of self-determination with all three of the basic psychological needs (autonomy, competence and social interaction) in play.
- The law of the customer: Agile working ensures that everyone working in a team has a clear line of sight between their role and the customer they serve.
- The law of the network: this law underpins the other two. This is because it views the organisation as a continually evolving, flexible network of teams that collaborate to delight the customer.

Agile is a cultural tool that takes leaders on a journey that is never-ending. This clues leaders to the notion that Agile is rooted in constant change. Agile does away with the linear approach of ensuing project phases in favour of working on data collection, resource allocation and product development simultaneously.

Table 4.1 Manifesto for Agile software development

Old	New
Processes and tools	Individuals and their interactions
Comprehensive documentation	Working software
Contract negotiation	Customer collaboration
Following a plan	Responding to change

Source: Denning, S., 2018. *The Age of Agile: How Smart Companies Are Transforming the Way Work Gets Done*. Amacom.

Because of the reduced development cycle, Agile working should bring products and services to market quicker, shorten the feedback cycle between the customer and team, and build teams of multi-skilled people. Research[8] suggests that 60% of firms adopting Agile working methods preserved their pre-pandemic performance during the pandemic, between March 2020 and March 2021. Data suggest that well-implemented Agile working practices result in higher employee job satisfaction.[9]

Over the years, Agile has started to move from software development to become an accepted mainstream business practice and has spawned a vast array of consultants eager and willing to train organisations and their members in how to implement it effectively. This is relatively comfortable for IT teams and new start-ups, but much harder (but still possible) for more established businesses, such as banks, that have strong compliance obligations and a heritage of working in a certain way.[10] As such, Agile is very definitely not a one-size-fits-all methodology.

Nor is Agile a standard HR intervention. Rather, it is a cultural shift that enables organisations to exploit the advantages of technology and big data. In the four types of corporate culture model (see Figure 1.3 in Chapter One), Agile represents a shift away from parent–child relationships (hierarchical) towards more adult–adult ways of working (egalitarian). This strongly suggests that the preferred cultural model for digital businesses is a hybrid of those corporate cultures that lie along the egalitarian axis (incubator and guided missile) or 'guided incubator.' In sum, it is not just technology that will help deliver strategic advantage but the deployment of Agile working as its cultural enabler.

DevOps

Developed from the core principles of Agile, DevOps means end-to-end automation in software development and delivery. DevOps arose because, in some traditional IT practices, every new feature must pass between differing teams, sometimes spending as much as 80% of the time waiting between them. Such time lags impede expedition of software. Furthermore, the business objectives may have changed during the development process, and the end product does not reflect this. DevOps reduces the gap between developers, operators and the end user. This is accomplished through improved tooling within a collaborative culture. There is no accepted DevOps process or methodology. Like Agile, it is a cultural intervention first and foremost and it differs from Agile as it has a stronger operational focus and works more flexibly in accommodating unplanned work. Both Agile and DevOps work optimally with full employee commitment. In this sense, they become an implicit way of conducting business and thus form an 'underlying assumption' of corporate culture, as discussed in Chapter One.

CREATING A MOTIVATIONAL ENVIRONMENT: ORGANISATIONAL LEVEL

MEANINGFUL WORK

There is nothing particularly new about the concept of meaningful work. As long ago as 1976, Hackman and Oldham's job characteristics model (JCM)[11] identified experienced meaningfulness at work as a critical psychological state that positively influenced intrinsic motivation. Within this context, team members can create meaningfulness for themselves, but this requires an enabling environment to do so. Research[12] suggests that meaningful work is a complex mix of the interaction of individual, job, and societal and organisational factors.

This provides one explanation as to why so many healthcare workers across the globe went above and beyond in their roles during the COVID-19 pandemic. It was not especially related to pay. Most were intrinsically motivated to work for a greater ideal. There are links here to transformational leaders who elevate the consciousness of their followers through appealing to higher ideals and values. Understanding this interaction of individual, organisational and societal factors is key for organisations who seek to foster meaningful work within their workforce.

People find meaningfulness in adverse circumstances or when working through some seemingly intractable problem. Other research[13] suggests that meaningfulness is rarely expressed in the moment but is rather a function of retrospective introspection concluding that meaningful work is 'complex and profound, going far beyond the relative superficialities of satisfaction or engagement – and almost never related to one's employer or manager.'

FOMENTING A SOCIAL IDENTITY

Most people would prefer to have a positive self-concept rather than a negative one, and thus it follows that they will seek to view their group affiliations in a positive light as well.[14] They will do this by comparing their affiliations with other groups. These comparisons are important because they contribute to our own self-esteem. Substitute 'group' for 'organisation,' and it is clear how this becomes relevant to retention. If the organisation is successful, employees can enjoy the reflected kudos of working in such a business, which, in part, might explain why retention rates at Apple are so high. Thus, because people have a need for positive self-regard, they will look for ways in which their ingroup (current employer) can be distinguished from the out-group (other organisations). It works conversely too. Should they start to view their organisation in a negative light that might impact their own self-regard, they may then be encouraged to look elsewhere for alternative affiliations. Virgin Atlantic makes much play of the difference between itself and rival airlines. This is heavily reinforced through its 2022 advertising campaign that invites viewers to see the world differently. Indeed, as its website attests, 'being brilliantly different is what we do. It's who we are. And we wouldn't have it any other way.' As noted in Chapter Two, the TV advertising campaigns frequently have a positive outcome in increased applications for cabin crew. As such, Virgin Atlantic is clearly differentiating itself vis-à-vis competitors not just for its flying experience, but also for the quantity and quality of talent that it attracts through developing a specific social identity.

There are clear correlates here with the employee value proposition (EVP) as described in Chapter Two. An effective EVP is not just an attraction tool gilded with worthy adjectives and verbs. To recall, the EVP should be distinctive, compelling, substantiated and relevant to current, as well as aspiring, employees. Identification with the organisation enhances loyalty and commitment, which in turn enhance employees' willingness to remain within the organisation.[15]

REMUNERATION AND REWARD

The central issue around money is that it is a dissatisfier rather than a satisfier. This is because the key point around wages and salaries relates to equity and fairness. For instance, an employee may receive what is perceived to be a salary appropriate for the role, but, if someone in a similar role is paid more, then pay becomes a demotivator. Thus, organisations that benchmark performance and pay better than market rates reduce the degree of dissatisfaction rather than enhance the rate of satisfaction.

Money is an extrinsic motivator. Intrinsic motivation decreases with extrinsic rewards. This is because the nature of the motivation changes. Some research[16] asserts that using rewards to change behaviour produces only temporary results. At its worst, it may implicitly generate bad behaviours in pursuit of monetary goals. The UK pensions mis-selling scandal is a good example of this, with many consumers, misled about the illegitimate nature of some financial schemes and trusting the advice that they were given, being mis-sold to.

Such theories contrast strongly with the belief system that monetary reward is a motivator. This forms part of the basis of sweet equity used by most private equity investors to incentivise senior employees by giving them 'skin in the game.' The overriding view is that it works for some occupational groups and work settings but not for others. For example, some research[17] in the UK public sector found that, although most staff agreed with the principle of performance pay, they believed also that it had improved goal setting. However, they also believed that it was divisive and inhibited group collaboration. Therefore, attitudes towards group performance pay were much more positive than those towards individual performance-related pay options.

Some employers, recognising the changing nature of work, are now offering additional benefits for long-serving employees to boost retention. For instance, Monzo, a challenger UK bank, will allow long-serving employees to take three-month sabbaticals. [18] Pay needs to be equitable, but employers need to adapt to changing times, and offering flexibility in work–life balance and attention to career development opportunities, if they were not before core retention tools, most certainly are now.

PERFORMANCE MANAGEMENT

Chapter Three noted that the digital revolution required new ways of thinking about the key behaviours that team members need to show to be effective in role. This has led to new approaches in performance management systems. How these impact goal setting, feedback and the emerging science of people analytics are now discussed in greater detail.

WHEN GOAL SETTING WORKS WELL

The basic premise of goal setting is that team members who are provided with challenging, but achievable, goals perform better than those given easy or no goals at all. It matters that these goals are specific. Setting goals that are not specific enough will make it hard for team members to evaluate their own progress against the target.[19]

They will only strive to achieve the goals if they believe that they have the capability to do so. In a practical sense, this is about having the necessary skills to achieve the goals. In a psychological sense, it is also about team members feeling that they have self-efficacy, which is team members' belief in their capacity to execute behaviours that drive performance. Team members with high self-efficacy will set higher individual goals than those with low self-efficacy. Success breeds success, and team leaders have a clear role here in building and sustaining team members' self-efficacy.

WHEN GOAL SETTING WORKS LESS WELL

When team members face a task that is overly complex, with ambiguous outcomes, then urging team members to do their best is likely to be enough. This is because raising the bar too high can increase levels of anxiety, which will inhibit task effectiveness. In short, team members may spend more time worrying about the task than executing it. Next, goal setting can be counterproductive in collaborations with creative people. This is because goal setting is perceived as an object of control, and control is an anathema to the creative process. Creative folk need a loose framework within which to guide their creative endeavour and careful and supportive feedback on their thoughts and ideas, especially in the embryonic stages of the creative process.

THE CRITICAL ROLE OF FEEDBACK

The best performance management systems and learning and development initiatives will be rendered useless without timely and effective feedback. Put simply: practice without feedback retards learning. Consistent findings across decades of research, however, suggest that employees do not receive sufficient effective feedback from their managers.

It is an erroneous assumption to view feedback as an acquired skill that requires little developmental investment. For example, some line managers may defer engaging in constructive conflict, which is often the currency of much feedback. They may not have been trained in how to give feedback sensitively and constructively. All this suggests that leaders should not be allowed to accrete learning by taking as role models others who may be less than effective at this! Training should focus on feedback on both technical and non-technical skills and recognise that the efficacy of the feedback is dependent on its content, quantity and quality and the manner in which it is given. Tailored development using role play and coaching skills sessions will ensure that leaders at least understand the core skills required to deliver effective feedback.

Frequent, systematic feedback has several advantages. It enhances ratings accuracy and has the potential to increase flexibility, and inefficiencies and flaws can be monitored and corrected rapidly. The more feedback the better. Some research [20] found that, on average, employees reported 3.8 feedback conversations over a three-week period. At high levels of frequency (more than ten feedback conversations), there was a further increase in job performance. This is because feedback improves the quality of the relationship between supervisor and employee, which in turn is related to positive work outcomes.

PEOPLE ANALYTICS

Chapter One noted the idea of big data as a strategic asset and introduced the emerging science of people analytics, defined as 'the analysis of employee and workforce data to reveal insights and provide recommendations to improve business outcomes.'[21] As noted in Chapter One, HR teams have not always welcomed this emerging science, fearing that the focus on quantitative outcomes risks their workforce being viewed as commodities rather than human beings with emotions, desires and needs. There are, however, no parts of HR that people analytics cannot offer substantial value if deployed effectively with appropriately trained team members.

People analytics range from the traditional data sources such as demographic data (e.g., age, gender, and employment history) and more fluid data (e.g., education level and absenteeism rates) to the more descriptive (e.g., turnover hotspots and appraisal data). The real business value resides in using the power of AI to move beyond descriptive and diagnostic analytics towards being predictive and prescriptive (as described in Figure 1.1 from Chapter One), thus giving insights to HR teams that enable proactive human capital management through delivering actionable insights to senior leaders. These data enable different questions to be asked of HR teams and the business − for example, ranging from the tactical 'what is our turnover rate?' to the more strategic 'what are the people factors that will improve business performance?' and 'which roles in the business deliver the best most value?'[21]

Advances in data collection technologies are expediting the ways in which performance can be monitored and evaluated automatically. Systems can now collate customer data from platforms such as Slack and Asana that enable collaboration. This requires new forms of data collection technology, and one such example is the use of sociometric badges. These are wearable electronic devices that capture both individual and team patterns of behaviour. In theory, these data should now enable analysts to determine the patterns of communication that deliver effective teamworking.[22] The implications for the future of performance management are clear to see. There are, however, clear ethical points to consider. Some organisations will feel that the constant monitoring and invasive inspection of team members' behaviours are against their culture. The ongoing issue as to what constitute 'personal data' under EU GDPR legislation may well impact take-up of this technology in European countries.

In summary, people analytic data can now provide a more comprehensive performance profile and accelerate the speed at which information can be analysed and acted upon. This will ensure that performance is more data-driven and objective. This is especially important when seeking to evaluate individual performance and behaviours conducted in team environments founded upon Agile or DevOps. Working optimally, people analytic data will deliver improved commercial value, enhancements to the employee experience and more effective organisation development.

TOWARDS A NEW DAWN IN PERFORMANCE MANAGEMENT

These technological advances allow for continual performance monitoring and real-time feedback to guide individuals and their teams to perform more effectively. This ability to track performance in real time is key. In today's highly dynamic and fluid work environment, instant data and feedback allow for quick course correction when 'stuff happens' or problems emerge from left field. Thus, AI and people analytics take ownership out of leaders' hands and empower teams to problem solve for themselves. IBM, for example, recognises that the lifetime of some skills is shortening quickly. It is therefore interested in technologies that can predict the future of work. Using AI, Watson Analytics looks at a team member's work experience to predict how their potential skills and qualities might best serve IBM in the future.[23] Watson also scans IBM's internal training system to assess if a team member has acquired new skills. Line managers can then take Watson's assessment rating into account as they make remuneration and promotion decisions. IBM asserts that Watson has a superior accuracy rate, compared with IBM's internal analysis with HR experts.

As such, the formal half-yearly or yearly appraisal process looks increasingly obsolete. Reviled by both managers and team members alike for its judgemental nature, backward-facing focus and heavy bureaucracy, modern technologies now enable a new performance management dawn that is more data-driven, adaptable and development-oriented. Digital businesses are at the forefront of this as they recognise that the team, not the individual, is now the relevant unit of performance, and the feedback loops inherent in Agile working should facilitate group problem solving in real time. Table 4.2 summarises the new dawn in performance management.

Table 4.2 The new dawn in performance management

From	To
Yearly/half-yearly review	Continual feedback
Backward-facing focus	Tracking performance in real time
Judgemental	Developmental
Bureaucratic	Flexible, adaptable and digitally enabled
Employing subjective ratings	Data-driven
Assessing individual performance	Developing individual contributions within the context of team performance

The case study in Box 4.1 is a practical example of how this new model is working.

BOX 4.1   CASE STUDY: LATTICE AND SENSAT

Lattice is a people management platform designed to assist the talent management strategy by connecting performance management, workforce motivation and career development in one unified solution.

Sensat is a software company which offers a visualisation and collaboration platform that helps project managers deliver infrastructure programmes to time and budget. Founded in 2017, the business has undergone rapid growth from an initial 20 employees to over 100 five years later. Within this expanding and fast-moving business context, the Sensat HR team had twin goals to both meet the strategic and operational goals of the business and 'make Sensat an amazing place to work.'

Performance management systems that worked well in the early years were now much less appropriate, and thus Sensat needed a more formalised process to ensure a consistent employee experience. Sensat deployed Lattice performance management platforms to deliver annual and mid-year reviews. Sensat also implemented Lattice's Goals and Feedback tools to ensure improved transparency around goal setting, measurement of progress and a culture of continuous feedback across the business that gave ownership of the feedback process to the individual rather than waiting for a mid-year or end-of-year review. The Lattice Grow tool linked performance management conversations to discussions on career pathways, thus signalling a shift away from a historical and judgemental mindset towards one that was future-focused and developmental.

Sensat now has a single platform that allows the HR team to scan across the organisation to build better employee experiences and make more informed, data-driven talent management decisions. For example, Sensat has achieved 100% completion of performance management processes and an enhanced insight into emerging people issues that, among other outcomes, have helped drive down attrition.

As organisations grow, so their culture needs to adapt too. To recall, Figure 1.3 in Chapter One is a two-by-two matrix of 'Four types of corporate culture,' and this case study is a useful example of an expanding business undertaking a cultural shift from a 'family' culture towards more 'Eiffel Tower' behaviours to embrace enhanced systems that help drive effective talent management actions across the business.

LINE MANAGER PERFORMANCE MANAGEMENT MOTIVATION AND SKILLS

The new dawn assumes that line managers can make the switch from tracking performance to actively coaching and mentoring employees to enhance their development. To echo previous commentary across this chapter, not all managers have the skills to do this effectively. Nor do they necessarily have the motivation to do it. This suggests that supervisor diligence is a key variable in the performance appraisal context.[24] It should not be assumed that all supervisors will see performance appraisal as an important aspect of their job. Just as we noted earlier that feedback is an acquired skill, so is the wider ability of senior leaders to manage performance discussions with competence and confidence, and this will frequently require appropriate development.

Agile organisations have already moved to more streamlined and less bureaucratic performance management systems. Some research[25] asserts that Agile organisations that link business priorities and employee goals (in particular, setting collective goals either as well as, or instead of, individual goals), invest in the development of their line managers' skills (in particular, focusing on frequent feedback and continuous conversations on development) and differentiate individual from team performance (based on attitudes, values and behaviours) are much more likely to design and implement performance management systems that employees perceive as fair.

Reducing the complexity of performance management processes will enhance the likelihood of full and proper participation by both line manager and team member. SMART (specific, measurable, achievable, realistic and time-bound) goals should be replaced by SIMple (specific, important and measurable) goals. Such goals should be the vital few (probably just three) to focus team members on what really matters.[26]

RETAINING DIGITAL TALENT

Analyses of employment trends in the USA[27] suggest that the tech workforce has been growing at a rate of 2.2% since 2001, which is well above the 0.4% average rise per year for total employment in the US economy. During the pandemic, this rise has continued unabated, while employment for all other occupations has contracted. This is not the case, however, across all roles in the tech sector. In the years between 2001 and 2021, computer and information systems manager roles showed an annual growth role of 2.9%, whereas electronics and electrical engineer roles showed a 3.4% drop over the same period. Similarly, mathematical and science occupations have grown at a faster pace than computer occupations, suggesting a strong demand for data scientists. The inevitable consequence of this is that the war for tech talent will remain as competitive as ever.

Employers are now having to work harder and faster than ever before to deliver digital talent to the business. There is no simple solution to this conundrum but, rather, a series of inter-connecting initiatives that will increase the chances of both hiring and retaining the quantity and quality of talent required to implement and drive digital innovation.

FIRST, LOOK INTERNALLY

Any number of research papers will conflate the hiring of digital talent with the need to attract and retain millennial and Gen Z workers. As noted in Chapter Two, this form of stereotyping is firmly rejected. Digital talent is, and will continue to be, deployed across the generations. Thus, businesses tailoring their skills training programmes to address their individual needs and aspirations will both increase the benefits of a multigenerational workforce and should form a core part of a business's talent acquisition and retention strategy. As such, it must pay first to look internally at the availability of talent who have shown a nascent interest in IT and who would be willing to explore further opportunities. Saville Assessment worked with Ricoh Europe to develop a programme to identify individuals to be placed on a digital talent programme who had the potential to move into new roles once they had completed the programme. Through a robust internal selection process supported by a comprehensive development programme, the business delivered 100 internal hires into hard-to-fill roles. The process also enabled those who were holding roles less in demand (owing to shifts in strategy) to transition into key roles and thus stay with the business.

BUILD RELATIONSHIPS

Some interesting research[28] into how businesses have constructed workplaces that drive effective performance in the digital era found that the winners in attracting and retaining digital talent aspired to relational rather than transactional co-ordination. In short, they focused on shared knowledge and goals and empowered them to build value for both themselves and their business. In this way, digital talent felt they were active participants in, rather than passive recipients of, their firm's talent management initiatives.

In addition, the organisations most effective at retaining digital talent were:

- accessing the gig economy to supplement their existing skill sets for specific projects
- developing highly connected workplaces (such as social systems, IT systems, networks and collaborative environments) so that gig economy workers could integrate seamlessly with current work projects
- co-ordinating efforts to facilitate knowledge exchange and informal learning between FTE and gig economy workers as part of normal working practice
- rather than lose team members to start-ups, creating innovation hubs where talent could work on their start-ups as well as keeping their relationship with the business
- supporting individualised and self-directed career management initiatives and fomenting a collaborative and high-performance culture that enabled all to deliver meaningful work

In summary, digital talent needs to be engaged in new and different ways that are relational (not transactional), offer informal (rather than formal) learning and development interventions and deliver meaningful (rather than repetitive) work conducted in workplaces that facilitate collaborative (rather than stove-piped) endeavour across the business.

DIVERSITY AND RETENTION

There are issues in the retention of minority team members within the technology industries. Despite the advance of technology roles over the past 20 years, there still exists a sizeable gender imbalance. In the USA, more than half the members of the workforce aged between 15 and 64 are female and yet they comprise just 14% of computer science majors. As such, the resolution to the issues is as much societal as it is organisational.

That said, there are some organisations seeking to make a difference at an early stage. For example, Cisco in the UK has developed a pathways programme that aims to inspire young people to consider a science, technology, engineering and mathematics career while simultaneously acquiring employability skills. This programme is a bona fide initiative to secure interest earlier in the school journey through engaging with students, typically at Year 7 (11–12-year-olds in the UK), before they select GCSE subjects or transition into work. There are some noticeable benefits emerging from this project – for example, enhanced engagement of both BAME and female students, improved confidence about their career aspirations and survey output that suggested 71% would consider an apprenticeship or job with Cisco. This programme will enhance its EVP as it positions the business as an educator and developer of people, which is an increasingly important consideration for someone both joining and staying in a business.

Other businesses are seeking to tackle the issue through reworking the traditional employment model to reflect the societies in which they do business and thus appeal to a broader range of candidates. The pandemic has delivered forms of working that give caregivers and others more flexibility in when, where and how they work and presents a window of opportunity for businesses to rethink how they can recruit and retain minority technologists.[29]

SUMMARY

The winners in retaining talent will be those businesses that create a motivational environment to ensure every role offers meaningful work, competence, autonomy and social interaction. They will set aspirational, but achievable, goals. They will foster a positive social identity for their business that people will feel proud to belong to. They will routinely benchmark externally to ensure that money does not become a dissatisfier. They will offer flexible working practices to those for whom work–life balance and career development are key motivators. They will grasp the nettle of people analytics and gather, harness and analyse people data that relate to business priorities. They will discard bureaucratic annual reviews in favour of tracking performance and offering feedback in real time. They will train and develop their line managers to manage performance effectively. They will retain digital talent through building relationships that transcend the mere transactional and focus on shared knowledge and goals within enabling environments that empower them to give of their best. Finally, they will work assiduously to improve the retention of minority group technologists through offering innovative programmes that support self-directed learning and career management opportunities.

RETENTION: TEN TOP TIPS CHECKLIST

We benchmark frequently to ensure remuneration levels that are at least compatible with the market	✓
We consult individually with every team member about changes to the workplace and their environment	✓
We understand that employees' continued tenure is linked to their self-concept	✓
We set challenging but attainable goals	✓
We retain digital talent through a focus on flexible employment within a team culture	✓
We design roles people want to do	✓
We recognise that teams are now the salient unit of measurement and design ways of working (e.g., Agile working/DevOps) to drive effective teamworking	✓
We collect and harness people analytic data that are valid and reliable and we use these to predict performance in role	✓

All our senior leaders are trained with the skills to manage performance that drive behavioural change	✓
We have designed a performance management approach that drives our business priorities and delivers results (e.g., it is a strategic business imperative not a compliance obligation)	✓

REFERENCES

1 : Randstad, 2021. Attracting and retaining talent, Available at www.randstad.co.uk/attracting-retaining-talent-2021/. Accessed 31 January 2022.

2 : Schaufeli, W.B., Bakker, A.B. and Salanova, M., 2006. The measurement of work engagement with a short questionnaire: A cross-national study. *Educational and psychological measurement,* 66(4), 701–716.

3 : MacLeod, D. & Clarke, N., 2009. Engaging for success: enhancing performance through employee engagement: a report to government. London: Department for Business, Innovation & Skills.

4 : Gifford, J. & Young, J., 2021. Employee engagement: definitions, measures, and outcomes [discussion report]. London: Chartered Institute of Personnel and Development.

5 : Deci, E.L. & Ryan, R.M., 2012. Self-determination theory, in Van Lange, P.A.M., Kruglanski, A.W. & Higgins, E.T. (Eds.), *Handbook of theories of social psychology* (pp. 416–436). Sage.

6 : Yukl, G., 1994. *Leadership in organisations* (Chapter 12). New Jersey: Prentice Hall.

7 : Denning, S., 2018. *The age of agile: how smart companies are transforming the way work gets done.* Amacom.

8 : Consultancy UK, 2021. Agile work helps firms successfully adapt to pandemic business. Available at: www.consultancy.uk/news/27310/agile-work-helps-firms-successfully-adapt-to-pandemic-business. Accessed 1 August 2022.

9 : Tripp, J.F. & Riemenschneider, C.K., 2014, January. Toward an understanding of job satisfaction on Agile teams: Agile development as work redesign. 47th Hawaii International Conference on System Sciences (pp. 3993–4002). IEEE.

10 : Birkinshaw, J., 2019. What to expect from agile? *MIT Sloan Management Review*, Special Collection, Staying Agile, 8–11.

11 : Hackman, J.R. & Oldham, G.R., 1976. Motivation through the design of work: test of a theory. *Organizational Behavior and Human Performance*, 16 (2), 250–279.

12 : Lysova, E.I., Allan, B.A., Dik, B.J., Duffy, R.D. & Steger, M.F., 2019. Fostering meaningful work in organizations: a multi-level review and integration. *Journal of Vocational Behavior*, 110, 374–389.

13 : Bailey, C. & Madden, A., 2016. What Makes Work Meaningful – Or Meaningless. *MIT Sloan Management Review*.

14 : Tajfel, H. & Turner, J., 1979. An integrative theory of intergroup conflict, in Austin, W. & Worchel, S. (Eds.), *The social psychology of intergroup relations*. Monterey, CA: Brooks/Cole.

15 : Fenwick, A., 2020. How to improve loyalty in a rapidly changing and digitized workplace. *Hult International Business School*. Available at www.hult.edu/blog/improve-employee-loyalty-in-digitized-workplace/. Accessed 16 April 2023.

16 : Kohn, A., 1999. *Punished by rewards: The trouble with gold stars, incentive plans, A's, praise, and other bribes*. Houghton Mifflin.

17 : Marsden, D. & French, S., 1998. *What a performance. Performance related pay in the public services*. London: LSE.

18 : Martin, B. 2022. Monzo allows employees to take three months' paid leave. *The Times*. Accessed 3 February 2022.

19 : Lunenburg, F.C., 2011. Goal-setting theory of motivation. *International Journal of Management, Business, and Administration*, 15(1), 1–6.

20 : Mertens, S., Schollaert, E. & Anseel, F., 2021. How much feedback do employees need? A field study of absolute feedback frequency reports and performance. *International Journal of Selection and Assessment*, 29(3–4), 326–335.

21 : Ferrar, J. & Green, D., 2021. *Excellence in people analytics. How to use workforce data to create business value*. London: Kogan Page.

22 : Pentland, A.S., 2012. The new science of building great teams. *Harvard Business Review*, 90(4), 60–69.

23 : Greenfield, R., 2018. Your raise is now based on next year's performance. Bloomberg. Available at www.fa-mag.com/news/your-raise-is-now-based-on-next-year-s-performance-39633.html?section=. Accessed 28 November 2022.

24 : McClendon, J.A., Deckop, J.R., Han, S. & Petrucci, T., 2020. A study of system execution of performance appraisal. *International Journal of Selection and Assessment*, 28(3), 322–336.

25 : Darino, L., Sieberer, M., Vos, A. & Williams, O., 2019. Performance management in agile organizations. McKinsey.com.

26 : Effron, M. & Ort, M., 2010. One page talent management: Eliminating complexity, adding value. *Harvard Business Press*.

27 : Barua, A., 2021. The tech workforce is expanding – and changing – as different sectors battle for talent. Deloitte Insights. Available at www.deloitte.com/xe/en/insights/economy/spotlight/tech-workforce-expanding.html. Accessed 7 February 2022.

28 : Dery, K. & Sebastian, I.M., 2017. Managing talent for digital. Twenty-third Americas Conference on Information Systems, Boston, MA.

29 : Lamar, K. & Shaikh, A., 2021. Cultivating diversity, equity, and inclusion. Deloitte Insights. Available at: www.deloitte.com/an/en/our-thinking/insights/topics/diversity-equity-inclusion/diversity-and-inclusion-in-tech/recruit-and-retain-experienced-women-in-technology.html. Accessed 2 August 2022.

DEVELOPMENT

INTRODUCTION

Sometimes, the concepts of training and learning and development (L&D) are used interchangeably. To be clear, training and development are planned activities designed to improve performance at the individual, team or organisational level. Learning is a permanent change in behaviour that is the outcome of practice or experience. Thus, much of learning is informal and unplanned.[1]

There might have been a time in previous decades where L&D was considered a secondary function within a business – a nice-to-have rather than an essential and the first to have its budget culled during difficult times. More recently, this belief has changed, driven by several socio-cultural trends.[1]

First, young people coming into employment look for opportunities to develop in role, and the opportunity for continuous learning is a prime motivator to join a business as part of a psychological contract between employer and employee.

Next, the effects of digitisation on work performance place a strong emphasis on the need for L&D professionals to ensure that the business has the required skills to understand both the nature of the technological revolution and how to maximise its benefits. Much learning can be accomplished online without the need for employees to leave their desks. This is part of an ongoing trend to put employees in charge of their learning, in place of the organisation.

Chapter One noted the rise of the gig economy and that many organisations now include these freelance workers within their talent base. Thus, they need to be accorded something like

DOI: 10.4324/9781003349587-6

the same opportunities for learning as full time employees. In this way, the business is investing in the skills of a key talent segment to ensure their continued relevance.

Finally, Chapter Four recognised the move to more team-based working as exemplified by the adoption of Agile working principles. This involves designing interventions to help people both learn as a team and work effectively as a team to ensure that they can leverage the power of collective endeavour.

Within this context, the six objectives of this chapter are to:

- outline some of the key preconditions that need to be established for effective L&D to take place
- provide a refresher and an update on the psychological principles of applied human learning
- give insights into how to enhance digital knowledge and skills across the business
- examine the true state of leadership development in the digital age: what works and what does not
- emphasise the importance of team training – especially for digital businesses
- explore some of the challenges relating to D&I in leadership development

PRECONDITIONS FOR EFFECTIVE L&D

As noted above, effective learning and development are those interventions that lead to sustained changes in the knowledge, skills and attitudes of individuals that benefit themselves, their teams and their business. Some research has shown that four characteristics differentiate those organisations with the most effective L&D strategies:[1]

- senior leaders are committed to learning and development. It is part of the 'cultural DNA' of the business
- L&D is part of the business strategy and has a direct impact on company performance
- organisations are rich in feedback; they promote continuous improvement, calculated risk taking and learning from mistakes

- there is senior leadership commitment to ensuring that
  L&D is fully resourced

These are important because they position L&D as a cultural intervention and represent a move away from single event training initiatives towards a culture of continuous learning. The future for effective L&D lies in joined-up initiatives that place the learner at the centre of the experience and that deliver learning that is 'just in time, just enough and just for me.' A practical example of this can be seen in the case study of PwC's New World, New Skills discussed later in this chapter.

PSYCHOLOGICAL PRINCIPLES OF APPLIED HUMAN LEARNING

So, how do people learn? What are the main learning theories? How do L&D professionals optimise their L&D interventions to ensure that employees are motivated to apply their learning to the workplace?

BEHAVIOURISM

Early learning theories centred around animal learning and the belief that this was the result of strengthening the connection between a stimulus and a response. This is frequently seen in dog training where the dog handler issues a command, and, when the dog obeys, it receives a reward. Over a period, the dog learns to associate the command and the behaviour with positive outcomes. It works the other way too: if the connection is followed by negative reinforcement, then the strength of that connection will decrease. It is not the rewards per se that produce learning. It is the brain's response to rewards that does this. Thus, learning has a strong cognitive component.

COGNITIVE THEORIES

There are, therefore, challenges in extending behaviourism to the more complex human behaviour of skill acquisition. For example, it does not address the abilities of humans to problem solve logically, think creatively or embrace the abstract. Furthermore, learners should not be passive recipients of data from others. They have emotions and motivations to learn that extend beyond mere reward. There are many and varied theories on the cognitive approach to learning, and there are several good textbooks that summarise these.

One theory[2] that holds special appeal suggests that skill learning proceeds in two stages: declarative knowledge and procedural knowledge. Declarative knowledge is explicit and fact based. For example, the Pacific is the biggest ocean on Earth, and Mount Everest is the highest peak in the world.

Procedural knowledge is practically based. It is about how we use that acquired knowledge so that it becomes implicit and automatic. The example frequently used to describe this model is learning how to drive a manual car. The learner needs to know the facts (declarative knowledge). For example, there is a steering wheel, a gear stick, and brake, accelerator and clutch pedals. Learning cannot proceed without understanding what these all do. Thus, the learner needs to convert this declarative knowledge into procedural knowledge through composition. This is where many rules distil into one rule that, through repeated practice and feedback, becomes automatic and thus requires less cognitive effort to perform. This model is the theoretical basis for many intelligent tutoring systems. This is not to dismiss behaviourism. Some parts of it still hold relevance, such as the concept of repetition and the creation of measurable learning outcomes.

CONSTRUCTIVIST THEORIES

These state that learners construct their own personal meanings (or constructs) from prior knowledge or personal experience. As such, trainees will emerge from the same learning event with different views and perspectives. This is a useful theory for teaching people to problem solve effectively, as the learner needs a base of knowledge from which to both create and evaluate new ideas. It is markedly less useful if the learning need is to design an intervention where the outcomes need to be consistently applied. Constructivism itself is not a particular pedagogy, but it does emphasis the notion of 'discovery' learning and forms much of the basis for Daniel Kolb's experiential learning theories.[3]

SOCIAL LEARNING

All the above theories have much to recommend them, but they do not address the fact that, as human beings, we do not live or work in a vacuum. We learn best when we work in socially rich and culturally supportive environments. Models of social learning [4] built on constructivist theories suggest that we learn through our social interactions with others, including peers, teachers and instructors. As such, instructors should be designing learning environments that provide opportunities for discussion, collaboration and feedback. Some research[5] has sought to extend this by emphasising the importance of observing, modelling and imitating the behaviours and reactions of others; the development of the trainee's beliefs in their capabilities (self-efficacy); and the enhancement of learner motivation through goal setting. In practical terms, this provides further evidence for the value of cultural reinforcement in L&D where senior leaders consciously model culturally desirable behaviours for their employees to emulate. The idea of social learning has influenced the development of the theory of paragogy,[6] which emphasises the benefits of peer assisted learning – for example, the ideas that the L&D team are not just teachers but co-creators of the learning experience, and that employees need to learn both how to learn and how to support others in their learning.

These principles hold appeal for digital environments as they support the peer production and free sharing of content that promotes learning for everyone.[7] They also map on to social media applications and the democratisation of data and knowledge. Finally, they support andragogy (the method and practice of teaching adult learners) through emphasis on meta learning (learning how to learn).

NEUROSCIENCE AND L&D

All the above theories of how people learn have been established for some time. And they are, of course, still highly relevant to instructional design. However, Chapter Three introduced the notion of neuroscience as an emerging concept within selection, and this is also having a significant influence on L&D and challenging some long-standing beliefs on how people learn.[8] For example, there used to be a notion that our brains are defined by a limit to what we can accomplish. Neuroplasticity is the ability of neural connections within the brain to change, remodel and reorganise to adapt better to new situations. As such, our brains are not just determined by our genes but are also moulded by our interaction with the external environment, especially our educational experiences, and this process carries on throughout life.

There are several implications for the L&D practitioner. First, that it is now possible to train cognitive skills, especially fluid intellect (to recall from Chapter Three – the ability to reason and problem solve independently of previously acquired knowledge), using computer-based training techniques.[9] Next, that playing action-based video games can also improve attentional processing,[10] which suggests an enhanced role for the use of gamification in L&D interventions.

Such advances have led to a growing understanding of the relevance of neuroscience to organisational behaviour, as noted in Chapter 3, optimising leaders' brains will soon be a critical source of competitive advantage in the business world. If this all seems too far-fetched, then consider evidence from the USA's Defense Advanced Research Projects Agency's[11] neuroscientific approach, which identified how the brains of novices and experts look markedly different. This was practically demonstrated in training interventions to accelerate novices in the acquisition of marksmanship skills. In simplistic terms, this was achieved through identifying neurocognitive factors that predict marksmanship skill acquisition and then integrating brain monitoring capabilities into rifleman marksmanship training. Using a neurofeedback programme, novices rapidly learned how to create the expert brain state, with preliminary results suggesting that this technique improved the performance of novices at a faster rate than that of other treatment groups. To echo the point above, this may seem Frankensteinian to some, but the technology is out there, and there is no going back! It also reinforces the role of neuroethics, discussed in Chapter Three, to ensure that neuroscientific tools and techniques are deployed appropriately.

LEARNING TRANSFER

Data[12] suggest that less than 10% of training expenditure results in observable behavioural change on the job. Given that organisations in the USA alone spent over $92bn in 2021,[13] there are return on investment improvements to be made not just in the USA, but across the globe. Just how should L&D professionals ensure that what is learned is replicated in the workplace?

As such, learning transfer is everybody's role. From the L&D professional to the trainees, their co-workers and their line

Table 5.1 Key predictors of transfer of training

Predictor	Comment
Trainee characteristics	
Cognitive ability	This is still the single best predictor of training transfer. Those with higher cognitive ability will be more successful in processing, retaining and transferring their learned skills
Conscientiousness	One of the Big Five personality domains defined as 'strength of purpose and drive to goal accomplishment.' Goals can increase motivation to learn and allow trainees to assess their capabilities against acknowledged standards
Self-efficacy	Those trainees who believe in their own capabilities will be more likely to transfer their training to achieve desired performance
Trainee motivation	Those trainees motivated to want to learn, who perceive training as useful and who believe that training will lead to positive outcomes are more likely to achieve enhanced transfer
Voluntary participation	Those attending training on a voluntary (rather than a mandatory) basis will be more likely to achieve enhanced transfer

Predictor	Comment
Training design	
Realistic training environments	Replicating the conditions that look and feel like the workplace leads to enhanced transfer. This applies as much to low fidelity simulations such as role-plays as it does to high fidelity simulations such as flight simulators
Error management	Transfer is greater if trainees are provided with error management strategies and instructions, compared with those who just receive error training alone or who are prevented from making errors during the learning process[16]
Behaviour modelling	Providing opportunities for trainees to observe and practise the required behaviours increases their ability to retain and learn new skills. Transfer is best achieved when both negative and positive models are presented; when practice includes trainee-generated scenarios; when trainees set their own goals; when their superiors are also trained; and when rewards and sanctions are applied to their work environments[17]
Work environment	
Transfer climate	A supportive transfer climate includes creating realistic trainee expectations at the outset of the training; ensuring that the trainee has adequate resources to practise and develop the new skills; and ensuring that prompts are in built to cue trainees to use their new skills
Support	Both line manager and peer support have a positive relationship to transfer. Line managers should set goals around expected performance and what good/great looks like post training and give constructive feedback throughout the trainee's journey to acquire new skills and/or behaviours
Opportunities to perform	Training design should allow for the swift application of new skills in the workplace. Line managers need to give time to the trainee to practise their new behaviours, and such practice should be sequenced as soon as practical following the training event

Source: Adapted from Grossman, R. and Salas, E., 2011. The Transfer of Training: What Really Matters. *International Journal of Training and Development*, 15(2), pp. 103–120.

manager – all have a role to ensure that what is learned is carried over to the work environment. All L&D events should be based on thorough instructional systems design. Older theories of instructional design[14] are still applicable in the digital age!

One way of studying training transfer (the extent to which the learning that results from a training intervention is applied in the work environment and delivers meaningful change) is to look at it from three related perspectives – trainee characteristics, training design and the work environment. There is much research[15] in this area, and some of this is summarised in Table 5.1.

Just providing learning and development opportunities is no guarantee that such learning will be applied to the workplace and deliver desired changes in job performance. Attending to the conditions outlined in Table 5.1 will reduce the risk that critical training investment is needlessly wasted.

DIGITAL LEARNING: HOW EFFECTIVE IS IT?

There was a gradual migration pre-pandemic towards changes in how L&D was delivered. Digital learning was becoming much more commonplace as businesses sought more flexible learning options. Come the pandemic, this move shifted rapidly towards online delivery because face-to-face interaction was no longer an option. Data[18] suggest that, in February 2020, 36% of organisations used webinars or virtual classrooms. One year later, as the pandemic took hold, this had leapt to 51%. This may seem a welcome, cost-effective solution and part of a wider trend towards adoption of digital practices. But does it work? Just how effective is digital learning?

Research[19] published in 2010 found that, on average, students in online learning conditions performed better than those receiving face-to-face instruction. Further research[20] published in 2020 concluded that online teaching and learning had significantly developed to the extent that most of the learning strategies that show promise in the online environment are those that also influence effective learning in face-to-face classrooms. These include 'multiple pedagogies and learning resources to address different student learning needs, high instructor presence, quality of faculty–student interaction, academic support outside the class and promotion of classroom cohesion and trust.' Unique to online learning are user-friendly technologies, induction to online instruction, opportunities for synchronous sessions (i.e., where content is presented through digital media but where students can interact through raising their hands to comment or send a chat message to the entire class, another student or the instructor) and the use of social media. Just as with face-to-face learning, greater interaction with the course content is positively related to better course grades. This research strongly suggests that the modality of instruction matters much less than the quality of the learning design and delivery.

Post-pandemic, employees need to adopt a growth mindset to rethink how they add value given the shifting nature of work that goes beyond just course attendance and formalised training towards more flexible solutions that are continuous, experiential and explanatory. Businesses can stimulate this by encouraging employees to access relevant development and recognising those who do it well (e.g., who undertake development and change a behaviour in a way that helps to deliver a commercial goal). It also means that senior line managers function as coaches and mentors and take real time out to invest this in the learning of their team members. Research[21] suggests that the key differentiator between organisations who are starting out, someway there and setting the pace on their digital journey is not necessarily about the quality of their talent per se but more about how they are helping that talent to be better equipped to cope with the changing nature of digital transformation.

MOBILE LEARNING

More recently, the use of technology in learning has migrated from computers towards mobile handsets – especially those that have smartphone capability. This has led to the growth of mobile learning, also termed untethered learning, and many have seized the opportunity to use laptops, tablets, and mobile phones to access learning on the move and at a time and place that suit them. This does not spell the end of tethered learning – there is still a time and place for that. And some commentators[22] recommend a blended approach, as follows:

1   create opportunities for learners to use their mobile phones within the training room. This will enhance collaborative learning through capturing and sharing of content
2   design learning content that can be shared both within the training room and outside it. The mobile content should be interactive and challenging
3   help participants to make the best use of their content to discover, share and co-create content with fellow participants

Promoting the use of untethered technologies has clear pedagogic benefits, but there will still be those who are resistant to change. Such transitions work best within a positive transfer climate, as described in Table 5.1. To recall, this relates to creating realistic trainee expectations; ensuring the trainee is supported with opportunities to practice new skills.

ENHANCING DIGITAL SKILLS AND KNOWLEDGE

Many organisations find it hard to cope with the pace and rate of change in the areas of digital transformation, AI and data analytics, leading them to develop L&D interventions that over-emphasise skills that were important in the past but bear less relevance to what is required in the future. Research[23] conducted in 2019 identified seven key insights from organisations that have been most successful in developing and delivering meaningful L&D programmes and are summarised in Table 5.2.

Table 5.2 Seven key insights from organisations that have been most successful in developing and implementing strong L&D programmes

(1) Identify a north star	Establish an overarching goal that provides a clear focus for L&D decisions
(2) Establish a skills baseline	Conduct a stocktake of the current skills and capabilities across the workforce. Where are they now? Where do they need to be? And how to bridge the gap?

(3) Ensure alignment with strategic goals	Focus on the strategic goals of the business and the knowledge and skills required to deliver on these
(4) Upskill the L&D team and support them with the required resources	L&D professionals need to acquire digital and analytical skills within their teams and more specific knowledge around digital learning content, delivery and evaluation. Key to effective implementation is the execution of sound coaching and consulting skills
(5) Learning in the flow of work	Allowing workers to learn as they work and at their own pace enhances employee engagement. In short, learning is designed for everyone, all the time and everywhere
(6) Develop individualised learning pathways	There is a move away from the one-size-fits-all approach of standardised learning pathways to those specifically designed for individuals, their role, learning needs and career aspirations
(7) Adopt Agile methods to meet individual and business needs	L&D teams respond quickly to changing business priorities and deliver minimum viable product into the hands of users, then test and learn and upgrade as required

Source: Collings, D. & McMackin, J., 2021. The Practices That Set Learning Organisations Apart. MIT Sloan Management Review. Accessed 14 March 2022. https://sloanreview.mit.edu/article/the-practices-that-set-learning-organizations-apart/

These seven practices should not be viewed as exhaustive, but they do offer a basic framework for how L&D teams can more quickly address the rate and pace of business change through preparing for the future to deliver meaningful and individualised learning content for the workforce as and when it needs it.

Those businesses undertaking effective digital transformation recognise that people lie at its very heart. It is not the technology per se that creates value; it is how employees are motivated, trained and developed to use the technologies in innovative ways to deliver effective digital transformation. In an organisational sense, it is also about the culture that leaders instil into the business (as discussed in

Chapter One) and ensuring that the workforce is truly engaged so that there is complete alignment, from the shop floor to the executive team, on what the new ways of working will deliver.

In a more global sense, some organisations are now designing and delivering very sizeable L&D interventions to ensure that their workforce has the skills it needs to address the challenges envisaged for the future. One such example is illustrated in the case study in Box 5.1.

BOX 5.1   CASE STUDY: PwC

PwC is a professional services firm that recognises that upskilling is key. For it, 'this is about anticipating the right skills for the future, laying the cultural foundation, delivering modern upskilling programmes, and building a learning and development function with the right EdTech to deliver a vastly better return on upskilling investment.' In short, spreading digital knowledge and enhancing the skills that are required for the digital age.

With the mindset that 'together we can grow tomorrow's workers today,' PwC designed and delivered a key initiative in 2019 to drive the firm forward to the digital age. The New World, New Skills programme offered digital skills training to more than 275,000 employees worldwide that would encourage time-saving processes. The design process took four years.

Content was varied and included online resource hubs, podcasts and the creation of digital academies. Key to the effectiveness of this programme was that it was positioned as much as a cultural initiative as a learning one. Thus, team members were incentivised to participate through, for instance, the attainment of a digital acumen badge and team-based rewards for earning the badge, such as extra time off for holiday weekends. This initiative was positioned as a citizen-led innovation, and, to encourage this, employees could post ideas or share code and work together to boost productivity.

PwC asserts that 30,000 people participated in the digital academies, and that millions of work hours have now been automated.

Part of the reason for the effectiveness of this intervention was that it was fully resourced, with the firm committing $3bn to the programme. Of course, resources are just not financial, but the quantum of this investment is a clear cultural indicator of the critical commercial importance that the senior leadership attached to upskilling through this L&D programme.

UPSKILLING THE BOARD FOR THE DIGITAL AGE

There were many causes of the financial crisis of 2008, and the use of collateralised debt obligations by financial institutions contributed to the breakdown of banking systems. The question was asked: to what extent did board directors fully understand the use of this and other exotic financial instruments and the risk that they posed to their business? More than a decade later, much the same question can be levelled at boards now as they seek to make sense of changing business paradigms. Just how much do their members understand, and need to understand, to offer effective guidance to their businesses confronted with the rapid advance of digital transformation?

There have been cases where chairs have hired a non-executive director with specific digital expertise and/or appointed a digital director to the board. These are, however, just sticking plaster solutions. Boards need to be engaged at much deeper levels to elevate their collective consciousness of digital knowledge and transformation to ask the right questions of their management teams and to hold them to account.

Key to the attainment of this goal is shifting mindsets in the board through investing in board training on the commercial implications of key technologies, so that board members feel comfortable with both the concepts of digital transformation and the specialist language that surrounds it. For example, one board took its team off to visit Spotify in Sweden. The objective of this trip was less about emulating what Spotify has done and how it works, and more about understanding and reflecting on the impact of digitisation on its own business model, strategy, culture and values. One area of best practice is to put the board through an intensive training programme led by an external faculty or technology provider that focuses on the commercial implications of digital technologies within the business.[24]

In a similar vein, digital transformation requires competent executives to ensure that it is delivered to time, quality and standard. More importantly, it also requires data engineers and other technology specialists as these are critical roles in delivering transformation across the business. As such, boards have a responsibility to ensure that businesses have the talent bench strength to deliver the strategy. It is very much a board responsibility to oversee talent risks and to maintain the right talent oversight.

There is little research as to how digital transformation impacts board roles and responsibilities. That which does exist[25] foresees a blurring between board and executive responsibilities as new technologies introduce layers of complexity to business processes, with many board members feeling increasingly drawn into a broader, diverse range of issues than might have been the case in the past. This places increased pressure on boards and their executive teams to carefully reappraise their respective roles and responsibilities to ensure clarity, both internally for the business and externally for wider stakeholder groups. The same research recommends seven tasks that boards should do before the adoption of digital solutions to understand the impact of digital transformation on board processes, and these are summarised in Table 5.3.

Table 5.3 Actions boards should undertake to better understand the effects of digital transformation on board processes

Invest in learning about the latest current and proposed technological advances that relate to the business	✓
Create working parties to assess the risks and rewards of applying these to current board practices and processes	✓
Focus on the problem, not the solution! Be wary of shiny new technologies that may dazzle more than they deliver	✓
Work with the executive team to be clear on their respective roles and responsibilities when implementing new technologies	✓
Support the board with relevant training so that members have enough knowledge and skills to deliver effective oversight	✓
Develop processes and tools to assist management to assess the information that boards need to know to make best use of their time	✓
Engage with industry associations to provide best practice solutions on digitising board processes	✓

Source: Adapted from Srinivas, V., Lamm, R. and Ramsay, T., 2019. *Bringing Digital to the Boardroom. The Impact of Digital Transformation on Companies' Boards.* Deloitte Insights.

LEADERSHIP DEVELOPMENT

Previous commentary on transfer noted that less than 10% of investment in training resulted in observable change. This theme carries over into leadership development, a global industry estimated to be a $50bn business, but there is little evidence that this investment delivers improved leaders.[26]

Despite this disappointing backdrop, there is now much research to suggest that experience is a key variable in predicting managerial success. Those who had experience in working across a variety of roles and challenging projects fared better than those who had worked in a narrower range of roles.[27] Most development thus takes place on the job. The issue therefore becomes one of defining the relevant types of experience that will deliver the most benefit to both the individual and the organisation. Harlow Cohen[28] describes an equally weighted algorithm to define effective leadership development.

> Exposure to a variety of organisation-specific leadership challenges + tangible performance expectations + clear-cut learning agendas + cross-functional involvement and collaboration = leadership development.

This pithy formula has several attractions. It is highly practical and simple in conception, but perhaps too reductive. This is because other research[26] has suggested that four sets of interventions define leadership development programme effectiveness. These are described below and correlate closely with previous commentary across this chapter, as follows:

- **focus on behaviours** that are key deliverers of effective business performance (points 1 and 3 from Table 5.2)
- **make it an organisational journey** not just functionally specific. This is about ensuring that leadership development covers the whole organisation, as illustrated by PwC. Significant benefits of digital working are driven by working collaboratively across the business to break down silos and enable improved flexibility and faster responses to fast-changing organisational priorities
- **design for the transfer of training.** Learning in the flow of work (point 5 from Table 5.2) sequenced quickly by

practical application on the job ('Opportunities to perform' from Table 5.1) increases the probability that learning will transfer to the workplace.

- **provide an enabling environment for change to flourish.** This relates to applying the work environment principles from Table 5.1. As such investing in time for the learner to practise newly acquired skills in the organisation and receive quick and supportive feedback. The role of the line manager is key here, not just in setting out goals and performance expectations but also in acting as a coach – flexing between direction and facilitation as learner confidence and competence improve.

70:20:10

The conventional model in leadership development asserts that 70% of learning happens through on-the-job experiences, 20% from interaction with others – especially role models – and 10% through more formal education channels. Some criticise this model for lacking theoretical underpinnings, as the premise was based on interviews with successful executives. A more generous perspective asserts that there are correlations between this formula and the acknowledged and applied principles of human learning as discussed earlier in this chapter. For example, formal education (declarative knowledge) is then reinforced by on-the-job learning (procedural knowledge), supported by positive social interactions and role models (social learning) and further reinforced by constructive feedback and reward mechanisms (behaviourism). All of which may be one reason for its enduring appeal since it was first proposed in the 1980s.

The model can lead to misinterpretation though. Some may take the view that, if only 10% of learning occurs through formal means, then 'classroom' instruction should be axed. But this, as learning theory asserts, is a big mistake. How else will procedural knowledge develop, without its declarative base? It also misinterprets the theory as having three independent components, whereas 70:20:10 works interdependently. Thus, rather than dismiss this theory entirely, others have sought to build on it in different ways.

One approach of interest is the development of the on-the-job, social, formal (OSF) ratio.[29] This asserts that 70:20:10 cannot be a fixed ratio. It depends on the business, its strategy and culture and the prevailing business context. Now, 70:20:10 is reclassified as on-the-job (O), social (S) and formal (F). The OSF ratio is a flexible rather than a fixed entity. To give a practical example, a pharmaceutical business at the cutting edge of research will have a higher 'F' ratio (formal learning) than a retail business focusing more on 'O' and 'S.' This inherent flexibility within the OSF ratio is especially relevant to digital skills training, where nimbleness and responsiveness are key factors in delivering 'learning in the flow of work' as described in Table 5.2.

Leadership development is at a crossroads. And there are three powerful trends driving change.[30] First, networked learning infrastructures will replace more rigid, classroom-based instruction. Second, traditional executive programmes that focused on disciplines such as strategy and finance are being replaced by those that address people management skills such as communication and leadership and problem-solving skills such as data analysis and interpretation. The third trend reflects the increase in platforms that deliver on-demand, customisable learning environments and personalised content. The market for executive education has been freed up, allowing companies to curate the best-quality content, instructors and experiences rather than the best-quality programmes. As such, business schools are reworking how they offer value – for example, looking across departments and functions to offer interdisciplinary teaching and adopt the same interdisciplinary approach to develop partnerships across the globe.

TEAM TRAINING

Across the assessment, there has been a strong emphasis on the power of collaborative work, which is the cornerstone of Agile working and much work in digital businesses. This requires effective teamworking. This does not happen by accident or osmosis. It needs to be worked on continuously, and this process can be accelerated by effective team training. There is now an extensive body of research on this subject, mostly from the seven-year research project, the TADMUS (Tactical Decision Making under Stress) programme, sponsored by the U.S. Office of Naval Research. The interested reader is referred to any number of books and articles from this research, but the following points are especially relevant:[31]

- effective teams comprise effective team members; as such, individual competence precedes team learning or, in the vernacular, 'you cannot make a silk purse out of a sow's ear'
- key team behaviours (i.e., communication, co-ordination, mutual support) require intact team training that allows for the demonstration of these behaviours, practice and then feedback
- there is a cognitive component to teams as well; team members need to possess shared mental models about their task and their fellow team members' roles that they must process quickly to maintain performance under stressful conditions; effective teams communicate *less* because they learn to anticipate the needs of their team members and implicitly synchronise their activities to achieve a task
- guided practice (task simulation and feedback) that exposes team members to a variety of differing scenarios is an especially effective team training strategy

In conclusion, effective team training is not a social activity or 'bonding' ritual involving tasks that bear little relevance to everyday work. Rather, it is a professionally designed instructional event, based on a clear understanding of team tasks, skills and behaviours, that creates a context in which team behaviours and skills can be practised and learned.

DIVERSITY AND INCLUSION IN LEADERSHIP DEVELOPMENT

Over the past decade, there has been a significant expansion of training interventions designed to enhance D&I practices within organisations. Just how effective are these? One comprehensive meta-analysis[32] of the effects of diversity training on four training outcomes over time and across characteristics of training content, design and participants is summarised in Table 5.4.

Table 5.4 Summary of meta-analytic research into the evaluation of diversity training

Research outcome	Comment
Training is most useful when it is integrated rather than stand-alone	Situate diversity training as part of a well-considered package of diversity-related initiatives. Integrated initiatives signal to the organisation a commitment to diversity over and above a single stand-alone event
Voluntary attendance at diversity training may not be as effective as mandatory attendance	Voluntary attendance may be preferred by participants but may also lead training providers to 'preach to the converted.' Mandatory training seems more effective in delivering behavioural learning
Longer training interventions delivered improved learning outcomes over shorter interventions when the media options included multiple, rather than single, instructional methods	Longer training interventions give more time for contact. Greater opportunities for practice lead to enhanced skill development
Cognitive learning was a more persistent outcome than attitudinal or behavioural outcomes	This suggests that participants may understand much more about D&I but not necessarily change behaviours. Corporate cultures that address, support and recognise D&I provide the seedbed for these initiatives to flourish. All training interventions need a supportive cultural context to be effective
The proportion of women in the training group was associated with positive reactions to diversity training	There are data to show that women tend to be more receptive to diversity training initiatives than men

Source: Adapted from Bezrukova, K., Spell, C.S., Perry, J.L. and Jehn, K.A., 2016. A Meta-analytical Integration of Over 40 Years of Research on Diversity Training Evaluation. *Psychological Bulletin, 142*(11), p. 1227.

The finding that mandatory training seems more effective than voluntary participation is contentious, not least because one of the constraining issues in D&I training and development is that they can look and feel like a compliance objective rather than an opportunity to lead difference.[33] This is important because there is also research[34] to suggest that compliance-focused training has negative effects on management diversity and may negatively impact transfer, as indicated in Table 5.1. As noted in Table 5.4, integrated training is more effective than stand-alone training, and thus it will be more effective to consider how to embed D&I within all L&D interventions. In this way, it becomes a cultural rather than transactional learning experience; an integral part of how to do the job rather than a compliance-driven add-on. The focus for the L&D professional is thus to be clear about what specific D&I training interventions will deliver that more integrated L&D offers will not.

There is an acknowledged shortage of IT talent across the globe. Hiring more talent may not be easy, and thus the focus switches to internal talent development. One avenue of promise is to increase female representation in technical roles. However, there is a gender disparity in the Great Resignation, with proportionately many more women than men choosing to exit the workplace. There are many and varied reasons for this, but childcare – in particular, the lack of it and/or the cost of it – is a primary contributory issue. But there is also a feeling of a 'broken rung,' where women in entry-level roles are promoted at lower rates than men. For example, the gender gap for women in technical roles is sizeable, with only 52 women being promoted to manager for every 100 men. To address this issue, L&D could develop an intervention that enables early tenure promotions for women.[35] In line with the need to undertake more integrated approaches to L&D, this requires the interaction of three reinforcing enablers: skills (including behaviours that help the transition into team leadership roles); support (mentors, coaches and role models who openly support the progress of women into technical roles) and structure (inclusive policies to ensure that all employees have equal opportunity to advance through early tenure promotions).

SUMMARY

In summary, the growth of technology in learning has enabled the trend away from teacher-led instruction towards a more learner-centred approach. Technology is not a silver bullet. It does not make up for flawed needs analyses or poor instructional design. Such basics are just as important for digital learning as they have always been. The winners in L&D will be those who create and foment a culture of continuous learning and development across their business; ensure that their L&D interventions incorporate acknowledged principles of applied human learning and conditions for learning transfer; embrace digital learning technologies; enhance digital skills across all levels of the business; continue to offer challenging assignments; set up project secondments to stretch and develop senior leaders on the job; and ensure that D&I is embedded across all L&D offerings as a cultural initiative, rather than as a discrete intervention.

DEVELOPMENT: TEN TOP TIPS CHECKLIST

We design our L&D interventions to place employees at the centre of their learning	✔
We provide flexible learning solutions that are continual and experiential	✔
Our L&D strategy unequivocally aligns with our business strategy and is laser focused on those skills and behaviours that drive commercial success	✔
We don't throw the learning baby out with the digital bathwater – we acknowledge the continued relevance of older pedagogic theories and techniques	✔
We keep a watching brief for emerging pedagogic theories (e.g., neuroscience) that enjoy sound conceptual foundations and acknowledged learning outcomes	✔
We encourage learning in the flow of work: 'just in time, just enough and just for me'	✔
Our board members have enough knowledge of digital strategies and digital transformation to ask the right questions of the executive team and hold it to account	✔
We consider and use group development activities to reflect the collaborative nature of work in digital environments	✔

D&I is part of our cultural DNA and informs all our L&D interventions	✓
We ascribe similar levels of attention and effort to the formulation of our L&D strategy as we would to our formal budgeting processes and marketing planning	✓

REFERENCES

1 : Cascio, W.F. & Aguinis, H., 2018. *Applied psychology in talent management.* Sage. Chapter 15.

2 : Anderson, J.R., 1982. Acquisition of cognitive skill. *Psychological Review*, 89(4), p. 369.

3 : Kolb, D.A., 1984. *Experiential learning: experience as the source of learning and development.* Englewood Cliffs, NJ: Prentice Hall.

4 : Pritchard, A. & Woollard, J., 2013. *Psychology for the classroom: constructivism and social learning.* Routledge.

5 : Wood, R. & Bandura, A., 1989. Social cognitive theory of organizational management. *The Academy of Management Review*, 14(3), 361–384.

6 : Corneli, J. & Danoff, C.J., 2011. June. Paragogy. In *Proceedings of the 6th Open Knowledge Conference, OKCon 2011*, Berlin, Germany, June 30–July 1, 2011. *CEUR Workshop Proceedings* (CEUR-WS.org).

7 : Wheeler, S., 2015. *Learning with e's: educational theory and practice in the digital age.* Crown House.

8 : Howard-Jones, P. & McGurk, J., 2014. Fresh thinking in learning and development. Part 1 of 3. Neuroscience and learning. Chartered Institute of Personnel and Development.

9 : Jaeggi, S.M., Buschkuehl, M., Jonides, J. & Perrig, W.J., 2008. Improving fluid intelligence with training on working memory. *Proceedings of the National Academy of Sciences*, 105(19), 6829–6833.

10 : Caplovitz, G.P. & Kastner, S., 2009. Carrot sticks or joysticks: video games improve vision. *Nature Neuroscience*, 12(5), 527–528.

11 : Raphael, G., Berka, C., Popovic, D., Chung, G.K., Nagashima, S.O., Behneman, A., Davis, G. and Johnson, R., Adaptive Performance Trainer (APTTM): interactive neuro-educational technology to increase the pace & efficiency of rifle marksmanship training. Available at https://www.academ ia.edu/52863198/Adaptive_Performance_Trainer_APT_TM_Interactive_ Neuro_Educational_Technology_to_Increase_the_Pace_and_Efficiency_ of_Rifle_Marksmanship_Training. Accessed 13 March 2023.

12 : Georgenson, D.L., 1982. The problem of transfer calls for partnership. *Training & Development Journal.*

13 : Statista Research Department, 2022. Spending in the training industry in the US 2012-2021. Available at www.statista.com/statistics/788521/training-expenditures-united-states/#:~:text=Following%20a%20dramatic%20increase%20of,to%2092.3%20billion%20in%202021. Accessed May 30 2022.

14 : Gagne, R.M., Briggs, L.J. & Wager, W.W., 1988. *Instructional design.* New York: Holt, Rinehart, Winston.

15 : Grossman, R. & Salas, E., 2011. The transfer of training: what really matters. *International Journal of Training and Development*, 15(2), 103–120.

16 : Heimbeck, D., Frese, M., Sonnentag, S. & Keith, N., 2003. Integrating errors into the training process: the function of error management instructions and the role of goal orientation. *Personnel Psychology*, 56(2), 333–361.

17 : Taylor, P.J., Russ-Eft, D.F. & Chan, D.W., 2005. A meta-analytic review of behavior modeling training. *Journal of Applied Psychology*, 90(4), 692.

18 : Young, J., Gifford, J. & Lancaster, A. (2021) *Effective virtual classrooms: an evidence review.* London: Chartered Institute of Personnel and Development.

19 : Means, B., Toyama, Y., Murphy, R., Bakia, M. & Jones, K., 2010. Evaluation of evidence-based practices in online learning: A meta-analysis and review of online learning. Center for Technology in Learning, US Department of Education. Available at: www.ed.gov/rschstat/eval/tech/evidence-based-practices/finalreport.pdf?%20utm_source=WhatCountsEmail. Accessed 23 November 2022.

20 : Lockman, A.S. & Schirmer, B.R., 2020. Online instruction in higher education: promising, research-based, and evidence-based practices. *Journal of Education and e-Learning Research*, 7(2), 130–152.

21 : Kane, G.C., Nanda, R., Phillips, A.N. & Copulsky, J.R., 2021. *The transformation myth: leading your organization through uncertain times.* MIT Press.

22 : Wheeler, S., 2019. *Digital learning in organisations. Help your workforce capitalize on technology.* London: Kogan Page.

23 : Collings, D. & McMackin, J., 2021. The practices that set learning organisations apart. MIT Sloan Management Review.

24 : Huber, C., Sukharevsky, A. & Zemmel, R., 2021. 5 Questions Boards Should Be Asking About Digital Transformation. *Harvard Business Review.* Available at https://hbr.org/2021/06/5-questions-boards-should-be-asking-about-digital-transformation. Accessed 13 March 2023.

25. Srinivas, V., Lamm, R. & Ramsay, T., 2019. Bringing digital to the boardroom. The impact of digital transformation on companies' boards. *Deloitte Insights.* Available at www.deloitte.com/content/dam/insights/us/articles/4937_Bringing-digital-to-the-boardroom/DI_bringing-digital-to-the-boardroom.pdf. Accessed 13 March 2023.

26 : Feser, C., Neilsen, N. & Rennie, M., 2017. What's missing in leadership development. *McKinsey Quarterly.* www.mckinsey.com/~/media/mckinsey/featured%20insights/leadership/whats%20missing%20in%20leadership%

20development/whats-missing-in-leadership-development.pdf. Accessed 13 March 2023.

27 : Gabarro, J.J., 1987. *The dynamics of taking charge.* Harvard Business Press.

28 : Cohen, H.B., 2019. An inconvenient truth about leadership development. *Organizational Dynamics*, 48(1), 8–15.

29 : Whelan, T., 2018. 70–20–10 and the concept of the OSF ratio. Training Industry. Available at https://trainingindustry.com/blog/strategy-alignment-and-planning/70-20-10-and-the-concept-of-the-osf-ratio/. Accessed 13 June 2022.

30 : Moldoveanu, M. & Narayandas, D., 2019. The future of leadership development. *Harvard Business Review*. https://hbr.org/2019/03/the-future-of-leadership-development. Accessed 13 March 2023.

31 : Salas, E. & Cannon-Bowers, J., 1997. Methods, tools and strategies of team training, in Quinones, M.A. & Ehrenstein, A.E., *Training for a rapidly changing workplace: applications of psychological research.* American Psychological Association.

32 : Bezrukova, K., Spell, C.S., Perry, J.L. & Jehn, K.A., 2016. A meta-analytical integration of over 40 years of research on diversity training evaluation. *Psychological Bulletin*, 142(11), 1227.

33 : Sweeney, C. & Bothwick, F., 2016. *Inclusive leadership: the definitive guide to developing and executing an impactful diversity and inclusion strategy: – locally and globally.* Pearson UK.

34 : Kalev, A., Dobbin, F. & Kelly, E., 2006. Best practices or best guesses? Assessing the efficacy of corporate affirmative action and diversity policies. *American Sociological Review*, 71(4), 589–617.

35 : Griffiths, S., Kubalcikova, P., Shenai, G., Wright, C. & Gascoigne, A. 2022. *Repairing the broken rung on the career ladder for women in technical roles.* McKinsey.

6

CONCLUSIONS. SO WHAT? AND WHERE DO WE GO FROM HERE?

INTRODUCTION

The previous chapters have described how to recruit, select, retain and develop talent, and this chapter will share how these initiatives can inform a more organisational perspective of the quantity, quality and readiness of that talent. Within this context, this final chapter will:

- discuss the value of differentiation and what is meant by 'potential' and review some current thoughts on talent reviews and succession planning
- extract common themes from across the preceding chapters and suggest how these might continue to impact talent management in the digital age
- look to the future to assess how organisations, jobs and D&I might change and the implications of these changes for human resource management and talent management

DIFFERENTIATION

To recall from Chapter One, the talent management strategy will have identified an inclusive (everyone in the organisation is considered 'talent') or exclusive (a specific focus on 'highflyers') approach. For most businesses, the exclusive approach is the preferred option. This is because developmental resource is scarce, and it makes commercial sense to invest it where it will

DOI: 10.4324/9781003349587-7

deliver the best return, and that must be in people of high potential, more especially if they are occupying critical roles.

The most popular method of differentiation plots current performance against potential and often takes the form of the nine-box grid. This begs the question, what is potential? Is there a universally agreed definition, or is this specific to the organisation? And potential to do what exactly? Progress one level now and perhaps a further level in the future? There are many and varied definitions of potential across the literature, and the interested reader is referred to work by Silzer and Church[1] for a comprehensive summary. Some suggest that, because potential differs from performance, one can promote on the former regardless of the latter. This cannot be right. This is because sustained high performance must be an entry requirement to any high potential programme. To do otherwise is to devalue current performance as a desired outcome across the business in a way that will negatively impact that programme's credibility.

If Table 3.2 (Leadership competencies for the digital age) provides the model for high performance, then what might be the model for potential in the digital age? The evidence suggests that these competencies cluster around six core areas: three cognitive skills (problem-solving, creativity and innovation, and strategic thinking) and three interpersonal skills (leadership, emotional maturity and team working). There are similarities in headings with those behaviours shown in Table 3.2, but showing 'potential' takes these to another level. Table 6.1 presents a concise model of potential for the digital age.

SUCCESSION PLANNING AND TALENT REVIEWS

The chapter heading asks the questions 'So what?' 'And where do we go from here?' Ultimately, the focal point of talent management initiatives coalesces around succession planning and talent reviews. These are key to organisational effectiveness because research[2] suggests that poor or non-existent succession planning costs public companies $112 billion in market value. Succession planning is 'a structured process that involves the formal identification and preparation of potential successors to assume new leadership roles'.[2]

This definition is useful because it supports the notion that effective succession planning involves assessment skills (using valid, reliable metrics) to identify the right talent and L&D initiatives to ensure that talent has access to the right developmental support so that it can hit the ground running should a suitable role emerge. Jack Welch, who had a 40-year career at GE culminating as chairman and chief executive, expressed the view that, should a high-potential employee leave the business, then that role would be filled within eight hours. On one level, this is an explicit message to the business that no one person is bigger than the business. On the other, it is an implicit message about the quality of the succession planning process that delivers 'ready now' talent to the business.

The formal nature of succession planning stresses that there should be regular talent reviews led by top management, who both help to coach and develop team members but also take opportunities to teach in more formal leadership development programmes. It also stresses the importance of succession planning being a transparent process. Those designated as high potential need to know this status and that this status is temporary. People can and do develop in role, and others deemed as high potential can find that, under the spotlight of this status, their shortcomings soon become highlighted. In the author's experience, these are frequently people who enjoy high self-presentation skills (and use these skills to get themselves nominated to high-potential programmes) but who struggle to live up to their preconceived notions of superior ability. Or, put more colloquially, 'empty barrels make the most noise.'

There are two differing methods of identifying potential among employees.[3] The first is to inductively establish intellectual and behavioural criteria, which usually take the form of a high-potential competency model (perhaps a more fulsome representation of the six digital competencies described in Table 6.1), and assess against those behaviours. The next is to take a more deductive approach and ask senior leaders to select those whom they view as high potential and then plot them against the nine-box competency grid or a similar graphical representation. Their research concludes that this deductive approach is the preferred method, as any definition of potential is situational, and the strait jacket of a high-potential

Table 6.1 A concise model of potential for the digital age

Core behaviour	Behavioural indicators
Problem solving (managing and assimilating streams of structured and unstructured data)	• Enjoys elevated levels of fluid intelligence (seeks order from chaos; has flexibility in thought and responds adaptively to novel situations)
Creativity and innovation (rapid experimentation to reduce uncertainty and inform on customer acceptance of new ideas)	• Possesses a growth mindset • Scans for a wide source of data • Comfortable with both convergent and divergent experimental testing • Learns early – fails quickly
Strategic thinking (evolving to stay ahead of the competition)	• Enjoys long-term and holistic thinking capabilities • Seeks competitive differentiation through platforms as well as products • Creates two-way customer conversations that inform strategy in real time
Leadership (leading remote teams of geographically diverse peoples)	• Uses active listening skills • Works to high levels of cross-cultural competence • Enjoys elevated levels of 'agreeableness' (willingness to be open to the perspectives of others, and a preparedness to accommodate these in own thinking)
Emotional maturity (maintaining composure under stress and pressure)	• Resilient in the face of adversity • Controlling of own impulses • Projects a measured emotional response to change • Works to high levels of positivity and optimism

Core behaviour	Behavioural indicators
Team working (creating teams to drive digital transformation)	• Foments a culture of effective teamworking across the business • Champions Agile/DevOps initiatives • Encourages inter-professional working • Works to build social connections within the teams

competency model may not be flexible enough to accommodate this. If the deductive approach is preferred, then line managers' nominations and ratings must be challenged assertively by those also familiar with the high-potential candidate. Failure to do this risks line managers nominating favoured employees without relevant and supportive data.

EMERGING THEMES FROM ACROSS THE CHAPTERS

In seeking to draw some conclusions from the preceding chapters, several themes emerge from the book thus far, and some of these are summarised below.

BUILD UPON RATHER THAN DEMOLISH

There has been an implicit sense across the research that digital transformation sweeps away fusty and outdated concepts and ways of working in pursuit of a technological nirvana predicated on exciting new and emerging theories. This is not the case. Across the book, the case has been made to build upon those existing theories and paradigms that still hold value. For example, business model renewal has an intuitive appeal and reflects the dynamic nature of digital transformation. However, to recall from Chapter One, the science is clear that those businesses that replicate and renew perform better than those that just fixate, replicate or renew. Similarly, Table 3.2 (Leadership competencies for the digital age) lists old and new behaviours. These are not presented as dichotomies; rather, aspiring leaders need to cement the former and quickly acquire the latter to be truly effective in role, and the speed of this is dependent upon the time it takes to achieve digital mastery (see Figure 1.2). To recall earlier commentary from Chapter One, caution advises against moving too quickly. Leaders need to manage the tension between cultural continuity and digital transformation, so that team members are not discombobulated by too swift a transformation but are guard-railed by elements of a past culture that allows them to move forward with comfort and acquire the behaviours that will define the optimal culture envisaged for the future.

LOOK INTERNALLY FIRST

Chapter Two noted that recruitment should not be the automatic default once an employee has handed in their notice or if a new role is required. It may be the case that, somewhere within the business, lie people with latent career ambitions who, with the right motivation and appropriate learning and development, could fulfil the role well. This is especially the case for digital talent, and the Ricoh Europe case study (Chapter Four) is a good example of how to scan internally for hard-to-fill roles. The advantages to internal promotion include a reduction in risk of an incorrect appointment because the internal applicant already comes with a track record of skills and behaviours that are relevant to the business and is acculturated to the organisation. It also signals to employees that there are career opportunities within the business and implicitly encourages them to develop their skills. There are disadvantages as well. External talent frequently imports fresh and bright new ideas into the organisation, and the de-risking of an internal hire comes with the risk of excluding star external talent.

PERSONALISATION AND THE CHALLENGE OF SCALING UP

The notion of personalisation has been apparent across every chapter of this book – for example, in putting the customer (Chapter One), the applicant (Chapter Two), the candidate

(Chapter Three), the appraisee (Chapter Four) and the learner (Chapter Five) as the focal point of each initiative. The question arises as how to maintain this individualised approach while simultaneously scaling up to reap the benefits of digitalisation, but without riding roughshod over the organisation's EVP? One answer to this conundrum echoes the previous point, which is to scale at a pace with which the business feels comfortable and which it can absorb without risking discontinuity. This is much less about scaling per se and much more about building capability that creates a competitive digital business. Simply put, scaling as a strategy to hyper-boost the benefits of digitisation without building the talent to create it, support it and deliver it just courts disaster.

DATA EVERYWHERE

Each chapter has noted the exponential rise in data emerging from digitalisation. Data inform the algorithms that drive AI, and, as discussed in Chapter One, how data are gathered, harnessed, analysed and deployed requires a coherent data strategy. The profusion of data generated by HR and talent systems does not necessarily mean the reduction of HR roles. Recruiters will still be required to build personal relationships with prospective employees, but they do so now from a much better-informed standpoint. This is because data and AI have absorbed the repetitive tasks and liberated HR specialists to indulge in more meaningful and value-added activities.

The challenge for organisations is to find enough talent with the right data management skill sets. Just hiring the odd data scientist here and there is not going to cut it. Rather, it is a both educational and cultural task to ensure the business can embrace data and the combined rigours of analytical and statistical thinking. Data enable evidence-based decisions to be made on current and future talent imperatives. As noted in previous chapters, these data can be both structured and unstructured and come from virtually anywhere. The analysis of these and other people analytic data requires HR professionals to acquire and develop their own analytical skills to make the optimum use of data. This point is elaborated upon further in this chapter.

LOOKING TO THE FUTURE: THE CHANGING NATURE OF THE ORGANISATION

The commercial organisation as a vehicle to deliver on investment has been around for many years. The future of the organisation as we have known it and understood it may also change. Part of the reason for this is, as noted previously, a shift in the power balance between the employer and the employee, with the latter now very much in control. These are highly skilled and trained individuals who will seek out lucrative self-employment while simultaneously enjoying the benefits of a flexible lifestyle denied to their traditionally employed colleagues. Those IT professionals at the top of their game have a choice, and many are choosing to freelance. Organisations will have to adapt or change to attract and retain quality talent. Meaningfulness in work matters. This is because AI should have reduced the burden of boring and repetitive work, leaving employees more time to seek out meaningful activities that align with their own values, motivations and career interests. Some commentators[4] predict that, by 2040, half of the workforce will be, or will have been at some time in their careers, self-employed.

Others see organisations replaced by networks or collaborative partnerships as the means of how work is executed. This puts a significant emphasis on relationship building, understanding who is out there with the skill sets required. Leaders will now be expected to lead virtual teams whom they do not employ and whom they may not even know. This suggests that leaders need be not technical experts but skilled curators of expertise across disciplines to solve complex, multifunctional problems.

Winners will build relationships, offer on-the-job training and development to all, and engage the workforce at a social and emotional level. HR platforms will deliver real-time feedback on individuals, teams and their leaders, providing data not just for remuneration decisions but that feed into the needs analyses for future learning initiatives.

LOOKING TO THE FUTURE: THE CHANGING NATURE OF JOBS

There is a belief that jobs are becoming increasingly obsolete as a structural unit of work. They are being replaced by a focus on skills. The difficulty with jobs is that they standardise tasks at a time when the execution of work requires flexibility and responsiveness. Furthermore, the move to cultural initiatives such as Agile or DevOps requires skills, not job roles, as the salient units of work.

As is often the case, necessity is the mother of invention. And the pandemic forced businesses to reconsider current working practices and adopt newer, different and smarter ways of working just to survive. To do this, firms used AI and gig economy workers to disassemble jobs into tasks that created a new role or task.[5] Some businesses have taken this one step further through disassembling the tasks into skills that are then matched to current and future work-streams. Those organisations that prioritise the attraction and retention of independent workers and that treat them on an equal footing with FTEs will be those that differentiate themselves through the quality and quantity of their people.

There are clear advantages to these ways of working. They increase the ability to 'swarm,' which is to quickly align skill sets to address tasks. In this way, the employee is moving from task to task, offering his/her skill sets whenever they are needed and frequently working simultaneously on multiple projects. There are disadvantages too. This keen focus on skills may inhibit the development of new and different skill sets that enrich the work life of the employee and add value to the business. Platforms such as Gloat provide the technological foundation for these practices to work, but technology is only part of the solution. Thus, what were once jobs completed by employees now become FTEs and gig economy workers with specific skill sets, formed into project teams to manage a prescribed task, which are then disassembled once that task is complete. HR's role is to make this happen across the business. The interested reader is referred to two articles[5],[6] for a further understanding of this significant change to both work and existing talent management practices.

Next, AI frees people from mundane tasks to work that they should find more meaningful and thus more motivational. Job redesign is encouraging senior leaders to move away from a simple focus on task execution towards a much broader conceptualisation of how the job creates new sources of value for both the customer and the organisation.[7] This forms part of a move within digital businesses to focus as much on outcome as on output, where the latter is defined as a first-order (usually quantitative) end-product and the former as a second-order (usually qualitative) effect. An example might be the Apple iPhone, the output of which is to provide mobile communication and take pictures through a camera, but purchasing an iPhone also has an outcome as a style statement – an aesthetic product with a strong brand image.

All this requires a mindset change away from a reliance on steady state environments with predictable outputs towards a future state of mild chaos and rapid change, with a focus on the best tenets of design thinking (Chapter Three) such as empathy with users, modelling through prototyping and a tolerance for failure that leads to rapid learning and adaptation. Such a mindset change is not accomplished quickly and requires an integrative approach developed from an empowering vision from the top supported by specific L&D interventions that give the team members the time and space to acquire, practise and hone their new skills in the workplace.

LOOKING TO THE FUTURE: D&I

Across the book, the implications of diversity and inclusion upon talent management have been reviewed. As noted earlier in this chapter, the workforce and the customer base that it serves will become increasingly diverse, and leaders need to be comfortable relating to and working with those from diverse backgrounds. This leads some[8] to assert that fairness in treating people will now be defined as treating people how they expect and need to be treated according to their work, performance and personal value set, rather than treating everyone the same. The impetus for this change is coming from the adoption by HR of marketing-related principles such as customisation, segmentation and personalisation that combine to suggest that treating everyone the same will be an ineffective HR strategy.

For those businesses that seek to attract diverse talent, how they frame their messaging around D&I is important. Research [9] suggests that most organisations use the business case for diversity (diversity benefits the organisations because it positively impacts the bottom line) rather than the equity case (diversity benefits the organisations because it is morally fair and just). The problem with the business case is that it may very well alienate those whom it seeks to attract. This is because it increases perceptions among minority groups that they are being employed because of their identity or as 'a means to an end' rather than because they have talents and skills that will benefit the business. The research concludes that the equity case halved the adverse impact of the business case, but the best option was not to justify commitment to D&I at all. To recall from Chapter One, the core layer of the Schein culture model (underlying assumptions) emphasises that the behaviour becomes so implicit that most employees do not recognise it. It must be the objective of every organisation to drive the D&I agenda towards this cultural layer where it requires little or no intervention because it is culturally ingrained.

LOOKING TO THE FUTURE: HR

The challenges facing current HR teams are many and varied, but three stand out.[10]

- as noted above, shifting skills requirements suggest that rigid HR processes used to predict future skills will be replaced by more flexible processes that use data gathered from evaluating tasks and workflows to anticipate short-term changes to critical workflows
- next, the scarcity of available talent and increased turnover rates suggest that some key roles will go unfilled. In the short term, there may be opportunities to redeploy some tasks across the business. In the medium term, businesses need to experiment with creative resourcing models, as discussed in Chapter Two

- the employer–employee power dynamic: it is not for employers to dictate when and how work is executed. Employees have a choice now and will exercise that quickly if they feel that their voice is unheard. Both sides should agree the optimal ways of working, which should also include hybrid working solutions

Longer-term considerations include how to organise the HR function to better address the challenges posed by digital transformation and post-pandemic work practices. Joe Mullings, CEO of the Mullings Group,[11] asserts that talent acquisition requires the adoption of invasive, aggressive behaviours from recruiters building a hiring brand and a compelling narrative as to why a high-performing talent should consider joining the business. Simultaneously, HR will need to address a raft of new policies emanating from remote working and the restructuring of the workforce and all that this will entail. Mullings asserts that these are fundamentally different behaviours, and anyone who believes that they can comfortably coexist under the same leadership or function is 'dead wrong.' This suggests a split, with the talent acquisition team responsible to the senior leadership for all recruitment and selection activity pre-hiring, and HR responsible for all policies relating to employees post-hiring.

An alternative view proposes HR 3.0 as a compelling model. HR now becomes an agile consulting group the purpose of which is to drive creativity and innovation, data-driven change and transparency across the business. A seminal article[12] by IBM's Institute for Business Value suggests that, in a business world characterised by transformation and disruption, HR 3.0 should be the logical operating model. To deliver this model, the authors suggested ten key action areas, and these are shown in Table 6.2.

Table 6.2 HR 3.0: ten key action areas

Action area	Implications for the organisation	Impact
1: Measure employee performance continuously and transparently	Clear and continuous coaching and performance conversations are essential to proactively address workforce and performance issues	Very high

Action area	Implications for the organisation	Impact
2: Invest in the new role of leadership	The role of leaders requires new and different skills and behaviours. Predict strong leaders with analytics and invest in their development	Very high
3: Build and apply capabilities in Agile and design thinking	HR must be equipped to help design and manage Agile teams through operations, rewards, performance management and workplace productivity tools	Very high
4: Pay for performance and skills in a fair and transparent way	The old model of pay for tenure prevents growth, innovation and the hiring of top people	Very high
5: Continuously build skills in the flow of work	Employees and leaders must be learning all the time, with both formal and informal learning embedded in the culture coupled with capability academies for deep skills	High
6: Design intentional experiences for employees	Today's workforce expects meaningful employee experiences that are highly personalised and responsive to their needs and are constantly improved	High
7: Modernise your HR technology portfolio	The move to a cloud-based architecture enables speed, scalability and flexibility	High
8: Apply data-driven insights	People analytics is now essential to understanding, managing and continuously improving organisational performance	High
9: Re-orient and reskill your HR business partners	HR must function as strategic advisers, trusted coaches and data-driven problem solvers	High
10: Source talent strategically	Top talent can come from novel sources, so companies must look inside and outside to find the best hires to remain competitive	High

Source: Wright, A. Gherson, G. Bersin, J. and Mertens, J. *Accelerating the Journey to HR 3.0: Ten Ways to Transform in a Time of Upheaval*. IBM Institute for Business Value. 15 October 2020. Available at www.ibm.com/thought-leadership/institute-business-value/en-us/report/hr-3. Accessed 23 November 2023.

Those who have read every chapter of this book will be unsurprised by much of the content in this table. Yet it remains the case that only 10% of HR executives were living this model in 2020. Action areas 7, 8 and 9 require a fundamental rethink in HR systems, roles and the KSAs to execute them effectively. Cloud-based HR systems should support businesses with time-consuming HR processes by providing easy management of employee data, automated manual tasks and clear information to the organisation. They should provide employee-enabled tools with anytime and anywhere interconnectivity allowing employees to collaborate virtually even if working remotely or in geographically dispersed locations. The learning and development platform should enable employees to maintain the currency of their skill sets. All these systems should provide meaningful data back to the business, allowing appropriate talent decisions to be made.

Such changes will require HR professionals to acquire different skills. One of these is to develop knowledge and comfort in analysing and understanding complex data and the statistical analyses that accompany them. Some universities have already spotted this trend, and the University of Hull in the UK now offers a master's course in people analytics that includes modules on research methods, psychometric validation techniques, predictive modelling, text mining and data visualisation.

The HR business partner has now evolved to become a more strategic role. This requires an enhanced focus on consulting skills, data-driven problem solving and strong commercial acumen. This will see a deepening of commercial competence and skills, especially financial skills. In this way, HR professionals can analyse people analytic data to generate commercial metrics such as return on investment and be comfortable using other capital budgeting methodologies to determine the utility of their interventions.

LOOKING TO THE FUTURE: TALENT MANAGEMENT

Much of the same questions levelled at HR can also be asked of talent management. Where does the future of talent management lie? And how might this discipline need to change to be relevant to business leaders?

In the book *The End of Jobs* by Jeff Wald,[13] the author describes total talent management (TTM) as the notion that a business can organise all its labour resources (such as FTEs, gig economy, robots and drones) on a single platform. In the past, if there was a job to be done, then a case was put forward to hire an FTE to do it. Now, gig economy workers and FTEs merge to form part of the same talent bank from which resource is selected to address the task. The first default, therefore, is to consider automation first – what can be done by AI and robots better and quicker than humans? Selecting the right gig economy workers comes next, with FTEs reserved for those tasks that remain and that require creative, collaborative and more strategic thinking to execute.

To echo previous commentary in this chapter, this is about matching workers' skills to work, not jobs to work. It is the workers' KSAs, not their job role, that decide who forms part of what project. AI will decide who is best placed to do this work because it will be monitoring the skill sets required and the availability of talent to supply them and will present a cost-effective solution back to the business, as described in Table 6.3.

Table 6.3 TTM process

TTM process	
Step 1	Work is analysed and deconstructed into projects and tasks
Step 2	AI analyses the tasks and the availability of skills and costs required to deliver the optimal business outcome
Step 3	AI matches the task against the Labour Plane (another AI system that holds data on talent profiles, people analytics, robots and drones). The Labour Plane suggests appropriate resources (including training) to deliver the tasks
Step 4	Labour Plane delivers an Agile team that collaborates with other Agile teams and tracks performance and responsiveness towards task completion
Step 5	AI captures all relevant performance data while updating project management software to convert the task into an end-product. Simultaneously, the client is invoiced for work, and the accounts payable team is alerted to remunerate the works for the task

Source: Adapted from Wald, J., 2020. *The End of Jobs: The Rise of On-Demand Workers and Agile Corporations*. Post Hill Press.

This is not a pipedream. Work is happening like this right now. Businesses are harnessing technology to balance people, systems and tasks to deliver improved work outcomes. They are using business and people analytic data, agile teamworking and an expanded and skilled labour pool, all driven by AI to deliver business solutions.

AND FINALLY ...

There is a need to place the concept of talent into context here. Talent is only part of the solution towards creating a winning business. Indeed, there are those[14] who assert that a focus on talent per se only succeeds in making an organisation *equal* to the sum of its parts. What is required is a wider perspective to make the organisation *greater* than the sum of its parts. Evidence in support of this notion comes from research across 1500 organisations which found that organisation-level initiatives accounted for more than four times the variance in performance over the knowledge and skills of individuals. Within this expanded perspective, organisational culture plays a critical role. A winning culture for the digital age is simply one that helps businesses flex and adapt to market changes. It prioritises creativity and innovation, risk taking and continuous learning. Senior leaders understand these core behaviours and take every opportunity to model these and recognise and reward those who execute them well.

Thus, talent plays an important role in organisational effectiveness but not as key a role as other variables. This echoes previous commentary from Chapter One that, to recall, noted that winning organisations score well against the four foundation clusters of strategy, structure, culture and execution. Talent is one of four additional capabilities that help to secure winner status. It is part of the alchemy to drive a successful enterprise, but those who focus on talent to the exclusion of all, or any, of these foundation clusters will surely see their efforts founder.

From the invention of the wheel to the dawn of the Iron Age, the creation of gunpowder in the 9th century to Einstein's discovery that $E = mc^2$, technology has always changed the course of history. What distinguishes digital transformation is the rate and pace of change.

During the Anglo-Zulu War in South Africa in the 19th century, brave Zulu warriors, armed with spears and shields, defeated part of the British Army, armed with rifles, at the Battle of Isandlwana. Later, the numerically superior Zulus moved to attack a garrison of 150 troops at Rorke's Drift and were eventually repelled. This battle is recounted in the film *Zulu*. Towards the end of the film, the sergeant remarks to the commanding officer (CO) that, 'It's a miracle.' The CO replies, 'If it's a miracle, colour sergeant, it's a Short Chamber Boxer Henry .45 calibre miracle.' To which the sergeant replies, 'and a bayonet, sir, with some guts behind it.' In a sense, both the CO and his sergeant were correct. Technology may have won the day, but it still required motivated, trained and competent talent, working as a team, to achieve the goal. In short, it was the harmonisation of technology, people and process. It was always thus. And it always will be for those leaders seeking to manage talent effectively for the digital age.

REFERENCES

1 : Silzer, R. & Church, A.H., 2009. The pearls and perils of identifying potential. *Industrial and Organizational Psychology*, 2(4), 377–412.

2 : Groves, K.S., 2019. Confronting an inconvenient truth: Developing succession management capabilities for the inevitable loss of executive talent. *Organizational Dynamics*, 48(4), 100668.

3 : Effron, M. & Ort, M., 2010. *One page talent management: eliminating complexity, adding value*. Harvard Business Press.

4 : Zaino, G. 2020. Predicting the world of work in 2040, in. Wald, J., *The end of jobs: the rise of on-demand workers and agile corporations*. Post Hill Press.

5 : Cantrell, S. 2022. Beyond the job. Deloitte. Available at www.shrm.org/executive/resources/people-strategy-journal/summer2021/pages/feature-beyond-job-cantrell.aspx. Accessed 15 September 2022.

6 : Cantrell, S., Griffiths, M. & Jones, R., 2022. The skills-based organisation: a new operating model for work and the workforce. Deloitte Insights. Available at www.deloitte.com/us/en/insights/topics/talent/organizational-skill-based-hiring.html. Accessed 15 September 2022.

7 : Hagel, J., Schwartz, J. & Wooll, M., 2019. Redefining Work for New Value: The Next Opportunity. *MIT Sloan Management Review*.

8 : Ziskin, I., 2020. Predicting the world of work in 2040, in Wald, J., *The end of jobs: the rise of on-demand workers and agile corporations*. Post Hill Press.

9 : Georgeac, O. & Rattan, A., 2022. *Stop making the business case for diversity.* Harvard Business School.

10 : Gartner, 2022. Top 5 priorities for HR leaders in 2023. Available at www.gartner.com/en/human-resources/trends/top-priorities-for-hr-leaders-cpc-2?utm_source=google&utm_medium=cpc&utm_campaign=RM_GB_YOY_HRL_CPC_SEM1_TOPHRPRTY&utm_adgroup=145087863800&utm_term=hr%20priorities&ad=629054458258&matchtype=p&gclid=EAIaIQobChMI66en8sr9-gIVD9tRCh08PwT7EAAYAiAAEgK1E_D_BwE. Accessed 26 October 2023.

11 : Alder, M., 2020. The end of talent acquisition? Available at https://podcasts.apple.com/gb/podcast/the-end-of-talent-acquisition/id963756980?i=1000520348916. Accessed 8 October 2022.

12 : Wright, A., Gherson, G., Bersin, J. & Mertens, J., 2020, 15 October. Accelerating the journey to HR 3.0: ten ways to transform in a time of upheaval. IBM Institute for Business Value. . Available at www.ibm.com/thought-leadership/institute-business-value/en-us/report/hr-3. Accessed 23 November 2023.

13 : Wald, J., 2020. *The end of jobs: the rise of on-demand workers and agile corporations.* Post Hill Press.

14 : Ulrich, D. & Ulrich, M., 2018. Building talent and organisation culture: a winning combination, in Berger, L.A., and Berger, D.R., Eds., *The talent management handbook: making culture a competitive advantage by acquiring, identifying, developing, and promoting the best people.* New York: McGraw-Hill Education.

INDEX

Locators in *italics* refer to figures and those in **bold** to tables.